THE GOSPEL UNDER SIEGE

THE GOSPEL UNDER SIEGE

Faith and Works in Tension

by

Zane C. Hodges

SECOND EDITION
Revised and Enlarged

REDENCIÓN VIVA

Box 141167
Dallas, Texas 75214

Additional copies of *The Gospel Under Siege* may be obtained by writing to Redencion Viva, P.O. Box 141167, Dallas, TX 75214.

The cost is $8.95 per copy. Texas residents should add 8 1/4 % sales tax, or 74 cents per copy.

First Printing, 1981
Second Printing, 1982
Third Printing, 1984
Fourth Printing, 1986
Fifth Printing, 1988
Second Edition, 1992

Copyright © 1981, by
Redencion Viva

Copyright © 1992, by
Kerugma, Inc.

ISBN Number:
1-879534-00-2

TABLE OF CONTENTS

Cover photograph: Dave Edmonson
Graphic design: Martin Massinger

AUTHOR'S PREFACE
To the Second Edition

The Siege Continues

The first edition of *The Gospel Under Siege* proved to be extremely controversial. Few readers were neutral about it. By many readers, the book was gladly welcomed and warmly praised. By many others, it was vigorously rejected.

Clearly *The Gospel Under Siege* had touched a nerve in the evangelical community.

The Gospel Under Siege has been largely ignored by evangelicals who do not believe in the eternal security of the believer. This wing of the professing church (often called Arminian) was not the target of the book in any case. A much better book for them is Dr. Charles Stanley's volume entitled *Eternal Security* (Oliver Nelson, 1990).

Much of the opposition to the first edition came from readers whose theology could be described as Reformed, or Puritan. Historically Puritan theology has been marked by its heavy stress on the Old Testament law, both as a rule of life for Christians today and also as a means of testing the reality of a person's Christian conversion.

In this form of theology, the Apostle Paul's statements about the contrast between law and grace are greatly weakened. Those who oppose Puritan thought are quickly labelled as "antinomian" (= against law). In fact, one writer actually stated that this book should have been entitled "Antinomianism Under Siege"!

But the most serious error of much Reformed, or Puritan, thought is its complete redefinition of saving faith. According to theologians of this persuasion, simple belief in the truth of the Gospel is not enough. Such simple faith is condemned as "intellectual assent" or even as mere "psychological faith." What is required, they insist, is some "act of the will" that implies, or includes, some kind of commitment to obedience.

The result of this theology is disastrous. Since, according to Puritan belief, the genuineness of a man's faith can only be determined by the life that follows it, assurance of salvation becomes impossible at the moment of conversion. The history of Puritanism shows that assurance is also virtually impossible at any time before death. Those who claim to attain assurance in the Puritan way can only do so by closing their eyes to the enormous sinfulness of their own human hearts.

In teaching these things, Puritan theology violently separates faith and assurance. By doing so, it destroys the Biblical concept of faith and renounces the view of faith held by the great Reformers, Calvin, Luther, and Melanchthon. (See the endnotes for documentations.) This book, therefore, is an urgent call to evangelicals to return to reformational truth about faith and assurance.

But after all, the debate is not really about whose theology traces to whom. Instead, the bottom line is simply, "What saith the Scripture?" That is the issue and the only issue. And that is why this book is concerned - not with historical theology - but with the text of God's Word.

Let the reader, therefore, ponder the arguments of this book in the light of Scripture and under the guidance of the Holy Spirit. Let him weigh the discussions found in these pages in direct dependence on God. The reader does not need the "priests" of any form of theology to tell him what to believe.

The Holy Spirit can teach us God's truth. And *that* is a conviction which is distinctly reformational!

Zane C. Hodges
September 12, 1991
Glide, Oregon

PROLOGUE

Last night Jimmy believed in the Lord Jesus Christ as his personal Savior. This morning he is bubbling with a joy he has never experienced before.

On his way to work he meets his friend Bill. Bill has always claimed to be a Christian. He also reads a lot of books on theology. But Jimmy has never been too interested in theology up until now.

"Say, Bill," Jimmy begins, "guess what. I got saved last night! I trusted Christ as my Savior. Now I know I am going to heaven!"

"Hmmm," Bill replies, "maybe you shouldn't quite say it that way. After all, you don't really *know* that you are going to heaven."

"What do you mean?" Jimmy enquires. "The Bible says, 'Believe on the Lord Jesus Christ, and you will be saved,' and that's what I did."

Bill gives Jimmy a wise and knowing look. It is the kind of look all perceptive theologians know how to give the ignorant and the unlearned.

"But did you *really* believe? Maybe you just believed psychologically."

"What do you mean?" Jimmy is feeling a little depressed now.

"I mean," Bill continues sagely, "you can't know yet whether you have *real* saving faith."

"How can I know that?"

"By your works. You'll have to wait and see if you live a real Christian life."

Jimmy is dejected. "You mean that if I sin, I'm not a

Christian after all?"

"No, I don't mean that," Bill assures him.   "All Christians fail once in a while."

"But how much do they fail? I mean, how bad does it have to get before I find out I'm not saved?"

"Well, it can't get too bad for too long."

"But how bad? For how long?" Jimmy feels desperate.

"I can't tell you exactly. But a true Christian doesn't practice sin. If you find that you are practicing sin, that will show that you didn't have real saving faith to begin with."

"What if I do pretty good for several years and then things start going bad?"

"In that case, maybe you weren't saved to start with."

"Maybe? What do you mean by that?"

"I mean," Bill's tone is solemn, "you'll probably have to wait until the end of your life before you can be sure you are a true Christian. You have to persevere in good works, or your faith wasn't real."

"Do you think I can be sure before I die?"

"Maybe. Listen, Jim, I've got to rush to work. We'll talk about this some other time. Okay?"

"Yeah, okay. See you, Bill"

Bill rushes off. Jimmy is devastated. All the joy he had experienced since last night has suddenly evaporated. He is now filled with questions and doubts.

Jimmy has become a casualty in the siege of the Gospel!

CHAPTER

1

THE GOSPEL UNDER SIEGE

"Unless you are circumcised according to the custom of Moses, you cannot be saved" (Acts 15:1).

With such words the Gospel came under siege during the earliest days of the Christian Church. The claim made by these words created the first theological crisis in the history of Christianity. Nothing less than the unity of the faith was at stake. That unity was preserved only when the Jerusalem Council formally rejected this erroneous doctrine (Acts 15:24).

But the attack has been launched again and again down through the centuries and in no age more often than in our own. The specifics may vary widely, but the attack remains fundamentally the same:

"Unless you are baptized according to the Biblical command, you cannot be saved."

"Unless you persevere in good works, you cannot be saved."

"Unless you yield your life to the Lordship of Christ, you cannot be saved."[1]

But against all such claims, whatever their form or character, the true saving Gospel stands in profound and majestic contrast: "And whoever desires, let him take the water of life freely" (Rev. 22:17).

The Claims of the Judaizers

There is no reason to doubt that the Judaizers of Acts

15 claimed to be Christians. They could not have gotten a hearing in the church at Antioch if they had not made this claim. In fact, they probably presented themselves as representatives of the Jerusalem church. The words of the Jerusalem Council, "to whom we gave no such commandment" (Acts 15:24), suggest that the false teachers appealed to the authority of Jerusalem for what they taught.

Naturally this means that they admitted the necessity of faith in Christ. But they insisted on more than that. They claimed that salvation also required submission to the Mosaic law. Circumcision was just the first step in that submission (see Gal. 5:3). So the debate at the Council correctly focused on the issue of obedience to the entire law (Acts 15:5; see 15:24).

In the same way, most modern assaults on the Gospel do not deny the importance of faith in Christ. On the contrary, they insist on it. But to faith are added other conditions, or provisos, by which the basic nature of the Gospel is radically changed.

Often, a distinction is drawn between the kind of faith which saves and the kind which does not save. But the kind of faith which *does* save is said to be the kind that results in some form of outward obedience. By this means a willingness to obey becomes at least an implied part of conversion to Christ. "Saving" faith has thus been subtly redefined in terms of its fruits.[2]   In the process, the unconditional freeness of the Gospel offer is seriously, if not fatally, compromised.

The Sincerity of the Judaizers

Nowhere in Acts 15 is the sincerity of the Judaizers called into question. No doubt they were genuinely convinced of the truth of their doctrine. In all probability they had grown up in the Jewish faith. They knew that the Mosaic Law was ordained by God. It was easy for them to draw the conclusion that there could be no salvation apart from obedience to that law. But despite all this, they were still tragically wrong.

When the Council wrote that "some who went out from us have troubled you with words, unsettling your souls" (15:24), they were not necessarily condemning the motives of the Judaizers. But they *were* describing the effects of their doctrine. The believers at Antioch had been troubled by the words these men had spoken, so that their spiritual experience had been "unsettled."

Sincerity is no substitute for truth. It is the truth of God alone that can establish people's souls and give them a genuine stability in holiness. "For it is good," wrote the author of Hebrews, "that the heart be established by grace" (Heb. 13:9). And it is truly the grace of God itself, in all its splendid freeness, that can establish the hearts of God's people.

The Judaizers probably thought otherwise. Like countless others who have followed them in the Church, they may have feared that to preach a free salvation would lead to lawlessness and sin. To prevent this outcome, insistence on the law seemed to be a moral necessity. But Paul and Barnabas did not agree. And the Apostles and elders at Jerusalem sided with them. Peter himself declared: "But we believe that through the grace of the Lord Jesus Christ we have been saved in the same manner as they [the Gentiles]" (Acts 15:11, Greek).

Here lies one of the great truths of the Christian faith. The law could not guarantee "life" to men (Gal. 3:21). It was fundamentally a ministry of condemnation and guilt (Rom. 3:19, 20; 2 Cor. 3:6-9). Only the grace of God in Christ can bring eternal life.

But although the New Testament pronounces the law a failure in producing true holiness (see Rom. 8:3, 4), people continue to feel that the law's basic principle is the only workable one. From a human perspective, man will not live as God desires him to live unless he is threatened with uncertainty about his eternal destiny.

As popular as this notion is, however, it is false. It reflects a weak view of the power of God's truth to create a new creature at the moment of saving faith. It also underestimates God's capacity to transform the saved individual into the likeness of Christ. It hopelessly misjudges the comparative power of fear and gratitude as motivations for right conduct.   And beyond all this, it fails to take into account the powerful inspiration of goals that are centered in eternity itself.   That is, it neglects the doctrine of rewards.[3]

The Judaizers and Satan

Not one of these errors happens by accident.   True, they are natural to the soil of the human heart.   But their growth is encouraged by the Enemy of souls.   Paul understood, as few men have, that blindness to the Gospel is fundamentally satanic at its core.   He wrote:

> But even if our Gospel is veiled, it is veiled to those who are perishing, whose minds the god of this age has blinded, who do not believe, lest the light of the gospel of the glory of Christ, who is the image of God, should shine on them (2 Cor. 4:3, 4).

There is no mention of Satan in Acts 15.   But who can doubt that the Judaizers were serving his interests and aims?   Not consciously or wittingly, perhaps, but serving them nonetheless.   For if the Devil wishes to blind the unregenerate world to the Gospel, could there be a better stratagem than to confuse the Church about its terms?   If those who preach the Gospel are unclear, or even mistaken, about it, how shall they lead unsaved people to a knowledge of the truth?

The siege of the Gospel is not fundamentally a work of man, but a work of man's Adversary.   For this purpose Satan can employ his own agents or he can employ well-intentioned, but misguided, Christians.   The effects of the siege, wherever real inroads are made, is to dilute the Church's concept of the grace of God, to diminish her power in proclaiming the truth, and to hinder her growth toward real spiritual maturity.   It is no accident that Peter wrote: "But grow in the *grace* and knowledge of our Lord and Savior Jesus Christ" (2 Pet. 3:18; emphasis added).

So it is not surprising that the Apostle Paul is never more vigorous than when he is defending the purity of the Gospel. In writing to the Galatian Christians, to whom Judaizers also had come, he is completely uncompromising:

> But even if we, or an angel from heaven,
> preach any other gospel to you than what we
> have preached to you, let him be accursed
> (Gal. 1:8, 9).

The language is sharp, but it is a measure of Paul's jealousy on behalf of the true grace of God. He knew he was wrestling with supernatural principalities and powers, and not simply with men (Eph. 6:12).

Conclusion:
The Judaizers and Scripture

Of course, the Judaizers must have appealed to the Scriptures. The authority of the Mosaic Law rested in the written revelation of the Old Testament. But this appeal was misguided. It misunderstood the Old Testament itself as well as the new revelation which had been made through God's Son.

In a similar fashion, modern attacks on the freeness of the Gospel also appeal to Scripture. But these appeals constantly rest on a misunderstanding of the passages in question. There is often also a failure to face the plain meaning of the most direct statements about the way of salvation. The confusion that results is enormous. The consequences are calamitous.

In the pages that follow, attention will be focused first of all upon the absolute simplicity of the offer of eternal life. This offer furnishes the only grounds for real assurance of personal salvation.

Next, consideration will be given to some of the major texts that are thought to teach the necessity for, or the inevitability of, perseverance in good works. In the process, the inconsistency of these views with the real terms of the Gospel will be faced.

Additionally, along the way, some of the true motivations for godly Christian living will be underscored from the teaching of the New Testament.

No study of this sort could accomplish its goals without the ministry of the Holy Spirit in both writer and readers alike. The author prayerfully desires precisely this ministry to the glory of the Lord Jesus Christ.

CHAPTER

2

JOHN'S GOSPEL:
CAN I REALLY BE SURE?

Few questions are more fundamental than this one: Can I really be sure of my eternal salvation? Can I know that I belong to Christ and belong to Him forever?

If perseverance in good works is really a condition, or a necessary result, of salvation, the answer to this question must be: "No." At least it must be "no" until the hour of one's death. For only then will it be seen – if it can even be seen then! – whether the degree to which I have persevered is adequate to justify the conviction that I am saved.

It does not matter how the insistence on perseverance is expressed. The result is the same. If continuing good works are a co-condition with faith, then they are clearly indispensable to assurance. Even if they are only the inevitable outcome of true saving faith, they still become indispensable to assurance. That is, only the presence of good works in the life can verify the genuineness of one's faith.

Consequently, when the Gospel is so presented that the necessity for ongoing good works is stressed, it becomes a gospel that no longer can offer true assurance of eternal life. The individual who professes faith in Christ cannot possess, at the moment of faith, a certainty about his eternal destiny. Under some forms of theology, he cannot even be sure he has really believed![1] But this result is nothing less than a denial of a fundamental aspect of the Biblical Gospel.

Sometimes this tragic loss of assurance is concealed by the statement, "I *believe* I am a child of God." But this trades on an ambiguity in the English word "believe." The statement may mean, "I am *truly convinced* that I am a child of God." But it may also mean, "I *think* I am a child of God." A person who only considers it *probable* that he is a true Christian does not understand the New Testament offer of eternal life.

Assurance
Part of God's Offer

A careful consideration of the offer of salvation, as Jesus Himself presented it, will show that assurance is part of that offer.

One forceful example of this is John 5:24,

> Most assuredly, I say to you, he who hears My word and believes in Him who sent Me has everlasting life, and shall not come into judgment, but has passed from death into life.

Anyone who takes this statement at face value should be able to say, "I *know* I have everlasting life. I *know* I will not come into judgment."

But if assurance arises from a simple promise like this, it has nothing to do with works. To begin with, the statement of Jesus does not call for works. It calls only for faith. Moreover, the guarantee which He makes is relevant to the very moment of faith. "He who hears . . . believes . . . has . . . " On the authority of Jesus, the believer can know he has eternal life at the very moment he believes God for it.

The importance of this cannot be stressed too much. Assurance does not await the day of our death. It does not await the day when we stand before God in judgment. For in John 5:24 it is declared that, for the believer, there is *no* judgment. That is, there is no final assessment by which *his eternal destiny* hangs in balance. Already he has passed out of the sphere of spiritual death and into the realm of spiritual life.

It is precisely such a verse that confronts those who insist on works with an insoluble problem. If works are a co-condition with faith for eternal life, the Lord's failure to say so cannot be explained. But if works are a necessary outcome of saving faith, the problem is equally great. For in that case, one of two propositions must true: (1) the believer also knows at the moment of faith that he will persevere in good works, or (2) the believer does not know whether he has in fact truly believed.

Neither proposition can be defended successfully.

(1) Does A Believer Know In Advance He Will Persevere?

Not many would wish to maintain the first proposition. Although some believe the Bible teaches that a true Christian will persevere in good works, few believe that when a man trusts Christ he can know in advance that he will persevere in these works. The countless warnings of the New Testament against failures of every kind ought to be sufficient to show that such a guarantee is not Biblical. When Paul wrote to the Christians at Rome, he used these words:

> For if you live according to the flesh you will
> die; but if by the Spirit you put to death the
> deeds of the body, you will live (Rom. 8:13).

In the original Greek, the form of the conditional statements in both parts of the verse is exactly the same. The level of probability is the same for both. That two possibilities are placed before the readers is as clear as words can make this.

In reference to himself, as well, the Apostle recognized the possibility of tragic failure. In 1 Corinthians 9:27 he writes:

> But I discipline my body and bring it into
> subjection, lest, when I have preached to
> others, I myself should become disqualified.

In the face of a verse like this, it is impossible to maintain
that Paul possessed a certainty about even his own
spiritual victory. Obviously, this great servant of Christ
took the spiritual dangers he faced as grim realities. He
was motivated by these dangers to take care that he did not
run a losing race.

In neither of the passages just mentioned is there any
reason to find a threat to the believer's eternal security. A
Christian who lives after the flesh is certainly in danger
of death, but he is not in danger of hell. And to be
disqualified in the Christian race, about which Paul is
speaking in 1 Corinthians 9:24-27, is not the same as
losing eternal life.

More will be said about such matters in subsequent
chapters. For now it is sufficient to note that an
unqualified certainty about victory in Christian
experience does not exist. The New Testament cannot
correctly be said to offer a certainty like this.

(2) Does A Believer Not Know
Whether He Believes?

It is not surprising that most of those who hold that
works must verify faith adopt the second alternative.
This is not always done explicitly, but it remains the only
other option.

If a believer cannot be certain at the time of
conversion that he will live effectively for Christ, on the
premise that he *will* do so *if* he is saved, it follows that he
cannot know at the time of conversion that he is truly
saved. And since eternal life is offered to faith alone, then
it also follows that he cannot know whether he has truly
believed.

This view of things involves a psychological
absurdity. At the level of everyday experience, if a man is

asked whether he believes a certain fact or trusts a certain person, he can always give a definite answer. Even an answer like, "I'm not sure I trust that man," reflects a definite psychological state. What it reflects is an attitude of *dis*trust toward the individual in question.

On the other hand, when someone says, "I trust that person," he is expressing a state of mind of which he himself is thoroughly aware.

To claim that a man may trust Christ without knowing whether or not he has trusted Christ, is to articulate an absurd idea. *Of course* a man can know whether he believes in the offer of salvation or not!

The Bible everywhere takes this fact for granted. When the Philippian jailor enquired of Paul and Silas, "Sirs, what must I do to be saved?" (Acts 16:30), their answer clearly offered him certainty. The words, " 'Believe on the Lord Jesus Christ, and you will be saved, you and your household' " (16:31), invite a specific, identifiable response of heart. Having made it, the jailor could know he was saved. That he *did* know this is clear from verse 34: "And he rejoiced, having believed in God with all his household."

The seriousness of this issue must not be passed over. An insistence on the necessity or inevitability of perseverance in good works undermines assurance and postpones it, logically, until death. But this denial of assurance clashes directly with the clear intent of the Gospel proclamation. It flies in the face of the offer of eternal life made by the Son of God Himself.

Jesus and the Offer of Life

The lovely story of Jesus and the woman at the well of Sychar is a case in point. His opening words to her were simple and direct:

> "If you knew the gift of God, and who it is
> who says to you, 'Give Me a drink,' you would

> have asked Him, and He would have given
> you living water" (John 4:10).

This is perfectly plain. If the woman had asked, Jesus *"would have given"* her *"living water."* Obviously, she could have certainty about the result of this transaction.

It should be observed that the transaction of which our Lord speaks is a definitive and unrepeatable one. A few moments later He tells the woman:

> "Whoever drinks of this water [from the well]
> will thirst again, but whoever drinks of the
> water that I shall give him will never thirst"
> (John 4:13, 14).

The Greek phrase translated by "will never thirst" is a highly emphatic one. It might be translated, "will by no means thirst forever."

According to Jesus, the need which this water meets can never recur. This fact clearly shows the eternal security of the believer. For if a person could lose eternal life, he would obviously thirst again. But according to the Savior's words, that experience is an eternal impossibility.

It is hard not to be impressed with the magnificent simplicity of the offer Jesus makes to this sinful Samaritan woman. Its very lack of complication is part of its grandeur. It is all a matter of giving and receiving and no other conditions are attached.[2]

The story is an illustration in narrative form of the truth expressed in Revelation 22:17, "Whoever desires, let him take the water of life freely." There is no effort to extract from the woman a promise to correct her immoral life. If she wants this water, she can have it. It is free!

If the mind of man draws back from so daring an expression of divine generosity, it draws back from the Gospel itself. If it should be thought necessary to add some built-in guarantee that the woman would not continue her sexual misconduct – and, according to Jesus, she was currently engaged in adultery (4:18) – that guarantee would be a false addition to the words of our Lord Himself. The result could only be a false gospel.

It must be emphasized that there is no call here for surrender, submission, acknowledgement of Christ's Lordship, or anything else of this kind. A gift is being offered to one totally unworthy of God's favor. And to get it, the woman is required to make no commitment for the future whatsoever. The water of life is free. It is precisely this impressive fact that distinguishes the true Gospel from all its counterfeits.

Did the woman therefore simply return to her former sinful lifestyle? The Scripture does not tell us. It is not at all the point of the story. But those who think that some promise from her, expressed or implied, would have guaranteed that she did not, have an unjustified confidence in human commitments.

Such an opinion would also reflect a lack of understanding about the strength of habitual sin. The bestowal of a superlatively valuable gift as an act of unconditional generosity was precisely the kind of action most likely to woo her from her former ways. It is more likely by far to have accomplished this result than any legalistic commitment into which she might have entered.

The woman *was* grateful. Her testimony to the men proves that (4:28, 29). And Jesus had disapproved of her life (4:17, 18). There could be no more promising start than that.

But her assurance did not rest on what she might later do. It rested instead upon the uncomplicated promise of the Son of God Himself.

The Free Gift in Paul

Naturally it is not only in the Gospel of John that the experience of salvation is seen as an unmerited gift. Paul also saw things this way. He writes:

For by grace you have been saved through

> faith, and that not of yourselves; it is the gift
> of God, not of works, lest anyone should
> boast. (Eph. 2:8, 9)

Here too, of course, assurance is plainly implied in the Apostle's words, since Paul directly declares that the readership is saved and obviously takes it for granted that they know this.   Moreover, this fact is not based in any way on their works but simply on God's grace and their faith.   As with the woman at the well, the reception of a gift is the basic issue. The Ephesians are clearly aware of having received that gift.

Even when Paul goes on to state the importance of good works, the appeal is founded on the fact that the readers are the product of God's saving activity:

> For we are His workmanship, created in
> Christ Jesus for good works, which God
> prepared beforehand that we should walk in
> them (Eph. 2:10).

One point is clear here. Good works are not seen as the *evidence* that we are God's workmanship, but rather as the expected *result* of that workmanship. Whether this result will be achieved is not stated. But it is both reasonable and natural to expect it to be. Since we are new creatures in Christ, that is how we should live. We should fulfill God's purposes and walk in the works He has already prepared for us to do.

Plainly then, in Ephesians 2:8-10, good works are not the grounds of assurance at all.   On the contrary, *assurance is the grounds for good works!*

How strange that so fundamental a point should be so widely overlooked.   The firmness of any relationship is the true basis from which its proper fruits can flow. Even in ordinary life this is so. Would the relationship of a husband and wife be the same if they were not certain whether they were married or not? Would a son have the same response to his father if he were unsure of his paternity?

To ask such questions is to answer them. Accordingly, those who so present the Gospel that the believer remains uncertain about his salvation actually undermine the intended effects of God's grace. This fact compounds the seriousness of their error.

Simplicity in Gospel Preaching

In proclaiming the Gospel of the grace of God, therefore, simplicity is at a premium. The faithful preacher or witness will strive, with the aid of the Holy Spirit, to make the terms as clear as Jesus made them, or as Paul did.

These standards are high, but the inclusion of works-related conditions into the proclamation must be firmly resisted. Not to resist this is to lay ourselves open to satanic manipulation. It is he who wishes to blind men and to prevent their salvation (2 Cor. 4:3, 4).

How simple the Gospel really is can be seen with superb clarity in the greatest salvation passage of all. John 3:16 is perhaps more widely familiar to people than any other verse in the Bible. And justly so. But its content is prepared for by John 3:14, 15, which declare:

> "And as Moses lifted up the serpent in the wilderness, even so must the Son of Man be lifted up, that whoever believes in Him should not perish but have eternal life."

Jesus is speaking here to Nicodemus, a Jewish rabbi. The Lord's reference to the Old Testament gave this man a visual image which illuminated the offer Jesus was making. The passage was Numbers 21 with its story about the fiery serpents by which the complaining Israelites were bitten. Two verses in particular are worth quoting in full:

> Then the Lord said to Moses, "Make a fiery
> serpent, and set it on a pole; and it shall be
> that everyone who is bitten, when he looks
> at it, shall live." So Moses made a bronze
> serpent, and put it on a pole; and so it was, if
> a serpent had bitten anyone, when he
> looked at the bronze serpent, he lived.
> (Num. 21:8, 9).

Of special interest is the Old Testament expression "shall *live*," or, "he *lived*." It is plainly appropriate to Jesus' discussion of "life" in John 3. In the ancient narrative the bitten Israelite was asked simply to take a look at the serpent lifted up on the pole. This look alone sufficed to meet his need. "When he looked at the bronze serpent, he lived".

In the same way, Jesus means to say, He Himself will be lifted up on the cross, and the one who looks to Him in faith *will live*. Could anything be more profoundly simple than that? Eternal life for one look of faith! Clearly, here too we meet the unconditional gift which may be acquired by any who desire it.[3] "Whoever desires, let him take the water of life freely" (Rev. 22:17).

It was after these words (3:14, 15) that the Savior went on to express the most fruitful declaration ever made in the history of man:

> "For God so loved the world that He gave His
> only begotten Son, that whoever believes in
> Him should not perish but have everlasting
> life" (John 3:16).

The number of people who have found the assurance of salvation in these words defies all computation.

And assurance is precisely what one *should* find in them. There is no mention of works. Faith alone is the one condition upon which a man may acquire everlasting life. Moreover, this secures him from perishing.

Indeed, if anyone who ever trusted Jesus for eternal life subsequently perished, John 3:16 would be false.

"Whoever believes" is as broad as it can possibly be and is wholly unqualified by any other condition.

Those who wish to qualify it, in fact deny it.[4]

Conclusion:
Simple Faith Saves

There is no question in John 3 of "this kind of faith" versus "that kind of faith," or "a faith which leads to this rather than to that." Still less is there anything about "*psychological*" faith over against "*true*" faith.

Theologians may complicate the issue of faith, but faith is a simple matter in the Bible. It is nothing more nor less than taking God at His Word, that is, receiving "the witness of God" as true (1 John 5:9, 10).

Or we may say that faith is the inner conviction that what God says to us is true. It is "being *fully convinced* that what He has promised He" is "able also to perform" (Rom. 4:20-22; emphasis added).[5]

God promises eternal life to everyone who believes that Jesus is "the Christ, the Savior of the world" (John 4:42; 20:30, 31; 1 John 5:1). Individuals are saved when they are convinced of that promise and thus are sure they have eternal life.

So, in John 3, the issue is faith, or confidence, in Christ for eternal life. Will a man *look* to the Crucified One for eternal life, or will he not? The man who does, *lives!* By this very simplicity, the Gospel confronts and refutes all its contemporary distortions.

Yes, I really *can* be sure!

CHAPTER

3

JAMES 2:
WHAT IS A DEAD FAITH?

"Faith without works is dead." So spoke James in the second chapter of his epistle. His statement has been appealed to many times to support the idea that works are necessary for eternal salvation.

Sometimes the claim is made that unless faith is followed by good works, the believer loses eternal life. At other times, a more subtle approach is taken. If a professing Christian does not manifest good works, he was never a true believer to begin with. Whatever James is saying, however, it can be neither of these ideas.

Dead Faith Is Like A Corpse:
It Was Once Alive

The second view, just mentioned, is so forced and artificial that if it were not maintained by obviously sincere men, it might be called dishonest. According to this view, a dead faith cannot save. Therefore, if a man lacks the crucial evidence of good works, it shows that this is all he has *ever* possessed – a dead faith.

This flies directly into the face of the text. In James 2:26 the writer affirms:

> For as the body without the spirit is dead, so
> faith without works is dead also.

No one who encountered a dead body, whose life-giving spirit had departed, would ever conclude that the body had never been alive. Quite the contrary. The presence of a corpse is the clearest proof of a *loss* of life. If we allow this illustration to speak for itself, then the presence of a dead faith shows that this faith was once alive.

Nor is there *anything at all* in the entire passage to support some other conclusion. As elsewhere in the epistle, it is Christian brothers who are addressed (2:14; cf. 1:2, 16, 19; 2:1, 5; 3:1, 10, 12; etc.). There is *absolutely nothing to suggest* James believed that if a man's faith is pronounced dead, it must therefore always have been dead. The assumption that a dead faith has always been dead cannot be extracted from James's text. It is nothing more than a theological idea read into the passage.[1] It is also a desperate expedient intended to salvage some form of harmony between James and the doctrine of Paul.

But by distorting the true meaning of the text, this idea has given rise to immense confusion. This confusion has had a harmful impact on men's comprehension of the Gospel of God's saving grace.

James Believed in the Free Gift of Life

We should carefully observe that James, like all the inspired writers, believed eternal life was the gracious gift of God. This is made plain in a splendid passage in his first chapter:

> Every good gift and every perfect gift is from above, and comes down from the Father of lights, with whom there is no variation or shadow of turning. Of His own will He brought us forth by the word of truth, that we might be a kind of firstfruits of His creatures (James. 1:17, 18).

Anyone who is familiar with the words of Jesus, as

James certainly was, can surely hear an echo of our Lord in a statement like this. New birth is a sovereign act of God. It is one of His good and perfect gifts which comes down *from above.*

In fact, in the expression "from above," James employs exactly the same word that Jesus used when He told Nicodemus, "You must be born *again*" (John 3:7). The Greek adverb is *anothen* and means both "again" and "from above." No doubt our Lord deliberately selected it for His discourse with Nicodemus. The supernatural birth which He was describing is both a *rebirth* and a *birth from above.* The play on words which this involves is an effective one.

In James's statement about our rebirth there is also a strong emphasis on the sovereign will of God. "Of His own will He brought us forth. . ." James insists. This perspective recalls Paul's statement found in 2 Corinthians 4:6:

> For it is the God who commanded light to shine out of darkness who has shone in our hearts to give the light of the knowledge of the glory of God in the face of Jesus Christ.

Here, too, the sovereign act of God is stressed.

Neither Paul nor James intends to deny the necessity of faith. But faith, as we see it in the simple, direct statements of the Bible about salvation, is nothing more than a response to a divine initiative. It is the means by which eternal life is received.

Since this is so, it is proper that God Himself should be viewed as the sovereign Actor at the moment of conversion. It is He who wills to regenerate. It is His Word that penetrates our darkness. Salvation, we may say, occurs when the sufficiency of Christ for my eternal need dawns on my darkened heart. At this moment of believing illumination, I become a Christian.

So there is no reason to doubt that James and Paul were in harmony about the way eternal life is received. For both of them it is the gift of God, graciously and sovereignly bestowed. Only when we take this unity for granted can we really begin to understand the meaning of James's instruction about works.

Exposition of James 2:14-26

(1) Works and Grace
Cannot Be Mixed

The place to start is where James starts. In James 2:14 his famous discussion is opened with the words:

> What does it profit, my brethren, if someone
> says he has faith but does not have works?
> Faith cannot save him, can it?" (Greek.)

The translation just given is based on the original Greek and is crucial to a correct interpretation. The form of the question which James asks in the last part of the verse is one which expects a negative response. The expected answer, from James's point of view, would be: "No, faith cannot save him."

Anyone who holds that faith and works are *both* conditions for reaching heaven will find no problem with a question like this. In that case the question simply means that faith by itself is not enough. In fact, this is precisely what James says in verse 17: "Thus also faith by itself, if it does not have works, is dead."

But the problem comes when we try to harmonize this idea with the Apostle Paul's clear denial that works are a *condition* for salvation.

For Paul, the inclusion of works would be a denial of grace. He is emphatic on this point:

> And if by grace, then it is no longer of works;
> otherwise grace is no longer grace. But if it is
> of works, it is no longer grace; otherwise
> work is no longer work (Rom. 11:6).

It is hard to quarrel with this point of view! In fact it is impossible to do so. Paul's point is that once works are made a condition for attaining some goal, that goal can no longer be said to be attained by grace.

But in James 2, James plainly makes works a condition for salvation. The failure to admit this is the chief source of the problems supposedly arising from this passage for most evangelicals. We ought to start by admitting it. *And we ought then to admit that James cannot be talking about salvation* BY GRACE!

But instead of admitting these points, many interpreters dodge them. This is frequently done by trying to translate the question, "Can faith save him?" (2:14), by "Can that [or, such] faith save him?" But the introduction of words like "that" or "such" as qualifiers for "faith" is really an evasion of the text. The Greek does not at all verify this sort of translation.[2]

Support for the renderings "such faith" or "that faith" is usually said to be found in the presence of the Greek definite article with the word "faith." But in this very passage, the definite article also occurs with "faith" in verses 17, 18, 20, 22 and 26. (In verse 22, the reference is to Abraham's faith!) In none of these places are the words "such" or "that" proposed as natural translations.

As is well known, the Greek language often employed the definite article with abstract nouns (like faith, love, hope, etc.) where English cannot do so. In such cases we leave the Greek article untranslated.

The attempt to single out 2:14 for specialized treatment carries its own refutation on its face. It must be classed as a truly desperate effort to support an insupportable interpretation.

James's point is really quite plain: faith alone cannot save![3]

(2) Salvation for the
Believer's Life

But what are we left with? A contradiction between James and Paul? This is what many have candidly thought, and it is easy to see why.[4]If James and Paul are talking about the same thing, they *do* contradict each other.

But are they talking about the same thing?

In the opening chapter of the epistle, shortly after declaring his readers to be the offspring of God's regenerating activity (1:18), James writes:

> Therefore lay aside all filthiness and overflow of wickedness, and receive with meekness the implanted word, which is able to save your souls. But be doers of the word, and not hearers only, deceiving yourselves (Jam. 1:21, 22).

That this passage is analogous to 2:14 is easy to see. Here, too, James is affirming the necessity of *doing* something, and he clearly means that only if his readers *do* God's Word will it be able to "save their souls."

At first glance, this seems only to repeat the problem already encountered. But in fact it offers us the solution. The reason we do not see it immediately is due to the fact that we are English speakers with a long history of theological indoctrination. To us, the expression "save your souls" can scarcely mean anything else than "to be delivered from hell."

But this is the meaning *least likely* to occur to a Greek reader of the same text. In fact the expression "to save the soul" represents a Greek phrase whose most common meaning in English would be "to save the life." In the New Testament it occurs in this sense in parallel passages Mark 3:4 and Luke 6:9 (see also Luke 9:56). Among the numerous places where it is used with this meaning in the Greek translation of the Old Testament, the following references would be especially clear to the English reader: Genesis 19:17 and 32:30; 1 Samuel 19:11; and Jeremiah 48:6. Perhaps even more to the point, the phrase occurs again in James 5:20, and here the words "from death" are added.

By contrast, the expression is never found in any New Testament text which describes the conversion experience!

The natural sense of the Greek phrase ("to save your lives") fits perfectly into the larger context of James 1. Earlier, James was discussing the consequences of sin. He has said, "Then, when desire has conceived, it gives birth to sin; and sin, when it is full-grown, brings forth death" (1:15). Sin, states James, has its final outcome in physical death. But obedience to God can defer death and "save" or "preserve" the life. This truth is echoed also by Paul (see Rom. 8:13).

This understanding of James 1:21 agrees completely with 5:19, 20, where James says to his fellow Christians:

> Brethren, if anyone among you wanders
> from the truth, and someone turns him back,
> let him know that he who turns a sinner from
> the error of his way will save a soul from
> death and cover a multitude of sins.

On this attractive note of mutual spiritual concern among the brethren, James closes his letter. But in doing so, he manages to emphasize once again that sin can lead to death.[5]

It has been observed that the Epistle of James is the New Testament writing which most clearly reflects the wisdom literature of the Old Testament. The theme of death as the consequence of sin is an extremely frequent one in the book of Proverbs. A few illustrative texts can be mentioned:

> The fear of the Lord prolongs days,
> But the years of the wicked will be shortened
>   (Prov. 10:27).
>
> As righteousness leads to life,
> So he who pursues evil pursues it to his own
>   death (Prov. 11:19).

In the way of righteousness is life,
And in its pathway there is no death
(Prov. 12:28).

The law of the wise is a fountain of life,
To turn one away from the snares of death
(Prov. 13:14).

He who keeps the commandment keeps his
own soul [i.e., his life!],
But he who is careless of his ways will die
(Prov. 19:16).

It is clear that this is the Old Testament concept which furnishes the background for James's thought. A recognition of this fact clarifies a great deal. "To save the soul" (="life") is to preserve the physical life from an untimely death due to sin.

(3) The Development of James's Thought in 1:21-2:26

It is best to regard James 1:21-2:26 as a single large section in the development of the epistle. James 1:21 sets the theme. The readers, who are born-again Christians (1:18), need to lay wickedness aside and receive the Word of God as the agent capable of saving their lives. But they must understand (1:22-25) that this will only occur if they are *doers* of the Word and not mere hearers. To be a mere hearer is to commit the folly of looking into the divine mirror of truth and forgetting what it tells us about ourselves. Only the man who is a "*doer of work*" (1:25, Greek) can expect God's blessing on his life.

There follows in 1:26-2:13 some specific information about what a "doer of work" actually does. He controls his tongue, is charitable to the needy, and keeps himself pure from worldly defilement (1:26-27). Moreover, he rejects the spirit of partiality and favoritism which is so common in the world (2:1-13). That spirit is wholly inconsistent with his faith in the Lord of glory (2:1).

Instead of partiality, therefore, there should be true obedience to "the royal law according to the Scripture, 'You shall love your neighbor as yourself' " (2:8). In fact, love and its handmaiden, mercy, are standards by which the lives of believers will be assessed at the Judgment Seat of Christ (2:13). They should therefore "so speak and so do as those who will be judged by the law of liberty" (2:12). The reference back to 1:25 is obvious in the phrase "law of liberty."

In referring to judgment, of course, James does not contradict the declaration of John 5:24 that the believer does not come into judgment. There is *no* judgment for the regenerate person if by that term is meant a weighing of his merits in terms of heaven or hell. There is not even any charge that can be brought against the redeemed believer. He is *justified* before the bar of eternal justice, as Paul so plainly states (Rom. 8:33, 34). Thus there cannot be any trial at all to determine the believer's eternal destiny. God declares that a settled matter when He justifies.

But the New Testament *does* teach an assessment of the believer's earthly experience in connection with rewards, or the loss of these. (See 1 Cor. 3:12-15; 2 Cor. 5:10.) More will be said of this in a later chapter.

James 2:14-26 is the final subsection of the larger unit, 1:21-2:26. At 2:14 James returns to the thought expressed in 1:21 about "saving the life." Since he has insisted that "saving the life" is only possible when one is actually a "*doer of work*"[!], he wishes now (2:14) to oppose the idea that faith can substitute for obedience and accomplish the same saving result he had mentioned earlier (1:21).

(4) "Dead" Faith Cannot Keep
A Christian Alive (2:14-17)

Keeping in mind the concept of "saving the life by obedience," we can now look more closely at James 2:14-17. James writes:

> What does it profit, my brethren, if someone
> says he has faith but does not have works?
> Can faith save him? If a brother or sister is
> naked and destitute of daily food, and one of
> you says to them, "Depart in peace, be
> warmed and filled", but you do not give them
> the things which are needed for the body,
> what does it profit? Thus also faith by itself, if
> it does not have works, is dead
> (Jam. 2:14-17).

Can the fact that a man holds correct beliefs and is
orthodox "save" him from the deadly consequences of sin?
Of course not! The very thought is absurd. That is like
giving your best wishes to a destitute brother or sister
when what they really need is food and clothing (2:15-16).
It is utterly fruitless!

As a matter of fact, this kind of callous conduct on the
part of one Christian toward another is precisely what
James has been warning against (see 1:27; 2:2-6)! It
superbly illustrates his point. Such idle words are as
"dead" (ineffectual) as a non-working faith! So James
says, "Thus also faith by itself, if it does not have works, is
dead" (2:17)

It needs to be carefully considered why James chose
the term "dead" to describe a faith that is not working. But
the moment we relate this term to the controlling theme of
"saving the life," everything becomes plain. The issue that
concerns James is an issue of *life* or *death*. (He is *not*
discussing salvation from hell!) The truth which he has in
mind is that of Proverbs: "As righteousness leads to life,
so he who pursues evil pursues it to his own death" (Prov.
11:19).

Can a *dead* faith save the Christian from *death*? The
question answers itself. The choice of the adjective "dead"
is perfectly suited to James's argument. Just as the idle
words of some ungenerous believer cannot save his
brother from death in the absence of life's necessities, no
more can a non-working faith save *our* lives from the
deadly consequences of sin.

(5) An Objector Speaks
(2:18,19)

In 2:18-19 James introduces the words of an imagined objector.[6] The entirety of these verses belong to the objector. The response of James only begins in verse 20. This is shown by the words, "But do you want to know, O foolish man . . . "[7]

The literary format James uses here was familiar in ancient times from the Greek diatribe. The diatribe was a learned and argumentative form of communication. The two phrases ("But someone will say" [verse 18], and "But do you want to know, O foolish man" [verse 20]) clearly show that the diatribe format is being employed. These two phrases bracket the words of the objector in verses 18, 19. Elsewhere in the New Testament, this same format appears in 1 Corinthians 15:35, 36.[8]

Since the statements in verse 19 about the belief of men and demons are the words of the objector – not of James! – their use by commentators to make a theological point is totally misguided. But what does the objection mean? Since most Greek manuscripts read the word "by" in place of the familiar word "without" in verse 18,[9] the objector's statement may be given as follows:

> But someone will say:
> "You have faith and I have works. Show me your faith from your works, and I will show you, from my works, my faith. You believe that there is one God; you do well. The demons also believe, and tremble" (Jam. 2:18, 19, Greek).

The argument which these words express appears to be a *reductio ad absurdum* (a reduction to absurdity). It is heavy with irony. [10]

"It is absurd," says the objector, "to see a close connection between faith and works. For the sake of argument, let's say *you* have faith and *I* have works. Let's

start there. *You* can no more start with what you believe
and show it to me in your works, than *I* can start with my
works and demonstrate what it is that I believe." The
objector is confident that both tasks are impossible.

The impossibility of showing one's faith from one's
works is now demonstrated (so the objector thinks) by this
illustration: "Men and demons both believe the same truth
(that there is one God), but their faith does not produce the
same response. Although this article of faith may move a
man to 'do well,' it never moves the *demons* to 'do well.'[11]
All *they* can do is tremble. Faith and works, therefore,
have no built-in connection at all. The same creed may
produce entirely different kinds of conduct. Faith cannot
be made visible in works!"

No doubt James and his readers had heard this
argument before. It was precisely the kind of defensive
approach a man might take when his orthodoxy was not
supported by good deeds. "Faith and works are not really
related to each other in the way you say they are, James.
So don't criticize the vitality of my faith because I don't do
such and such a thing."

James's reply (2:20) may be paraphrased: "What a
senseless argument! How foolish you are to make it! I still
say that without works your faith is dead. Would you like
to know why?"

Verses 21-23 are James's direct rebuttal of the
objection. This is made clear in the Greek text by the
singular form of "do you see" in verse 22. This shows he is
addressing the objector. Only with the "you see" of verse 24
does James return to the plural and to his readers as a
whole.

(6) Justification
By Works (2:20-24)

In refuting the objection he has cited, James selects the
most prestigious name in Jewish history, the patriarch
Abraham. He selects also his most honored act of
obedience to God, the offering of his own son Isaac. Since

in Christian circles it was well known that Abraham was justified by faith, James now adds a highly original touch. He was also justified by works!

James writes:

> But do you want to know, O foolish man, that faith without works is dead? Was not Abraham our father justified by works when he offered Isaac his son on the altar? Do you see that faith was working together with his works, and by works faith was made perfect? And the Scripture was fulfilled which says, "Abraham believed God, and it was accounted to him for righteousness." And he was called the friend of God (Jam. 2:20-23).

Earlier in this discussion we said that we can best understand James's point of view by recognizing his harmony with Paul. That is extremely relevant here. James does not wish to deny that Abraham, or anyone else, could be justified by faith alone. He merely wishes to insist that there is also *another* justification, and it is *by works*.

Of course there is no such thing as a single justification by faith *plus* works. Nothing James says suggests that idea. Rather, there are *two kinds* of justification.

This point is confirmed by a careful reading of the Greek text of verse 24. When he returns to his readers generally, James says, "You see then that a man is justified by works, and not only [justified] by faith." The key to this understanding is the Greek adverb "only," which does not simply qualify the word "faith" but the whole idea of the second clause. James is saying: Justification by faith is not the *only* kind of justification there is. There is also the kind which is by works.[12]

Somewhat surprisingly, to most people, the Apostle Paul agrees with this. Writing at what was no doubt a later time than James, Paul states in Romans 4:2, "For if

Abraham was justified by works, he has something of which to boast, but not before God." The form of this statement does not deny the truth of the point under consideration. The phrase, "but not before God," strongly suggests that the Apostle can conceive of a sense in which men *are* justified by works. But, he insists, that is not the way men are justified *before God*. That is, it does not establish their legal standing before Him.[13]

In responding, therefore, to the kind of person who tried to divorce faith and works in Christian experience, James takes a skillful approach. "Wait a moment, you foolish man," he is saying, "you make much of justification by faith, but can't you see how Abraham was also justified by works when he offered his son Isaac to God?" (2:21). "Is it not obvious how his faith was cooperating with his works and, in fact, by works his faith was made mature?" (2:22). "In this way, too, the full significance of the Scripture about his justification by faith was brought to light, for now he could be called the friend of God" (2:23).

The content of this passage is rich indeed. It is a pity that it has been so widely misunderstood. The faith which justifies – James never denies that it *does* justify! – can have an active and vital role in the life of the obedient believer. As with Abraham, it can be the dynamic for great acts of obedience. In the process, faith itself can be "perfected." The Greek word suggests development and maturation. Faith is thus nourished and strengthened by works.[14]

It would hardly be possible to find a better illustration of James's point anywhere in the Bible. The faith by which Abraham was justified was basically faith in a God of resurrection. Referring to the occasion when that faith was first exercised, Paul wrote:

> And not being weak in faith, he did not consider his own body, already dead (since he was about a hundred years old), and the deadness of Sarah's womb. He did not

> waver at the promise of God through
> unbelief, but was strengthened in faith,
> giving glory to God, and being fully
> convinced that what He had promised He
> was also able to perform (Rom. 4:19-21).

Abraham had confidence that the God he believed in could overcome the "deadness" of his own body and of Sarah's womb. But it was only through the testing with Isaac that this faith becomes a specific conviction that God could literally raise a person from the dead to fulfill His oath. Accordingly, the author of Hebrews declares:

> By faith Abraham, when he was tested,
> offered up his only begotten son, of whom it
> was said, "In Isaac your seed shall be called,"
> concluding that God was able to raise him
> up, even from the dead, from which he also
> received him in a figurative sense"
> (Heb. 11:17-19).

Thus the faith of Abraham was strengthened and matured by works! From a conviction that God could overcome a "deadness" in his own body (=inability to beget children), he moved to the assurance that God could actually resurrect his son's body from literal, physical death. In the process of carrying out the divine command to sacrifice his beloved boy, his faith grew and reached new heights of confidence in God.

In this way, too, the Scripture that spoke of his original justification "was fulfilled." That statement (Gen. 15:6) was not a prophecy, of course. But its implications were richly developed and exposed by the subsequent record of Abraham's obedience. Abraham's works "filled it full" of meaning, so to speak, by showing the extent to which that faith could develop and undergird a life of obedience. Simple and uncomplicated though it was at first, Abraham's justifying faith had potential ramifications which only his works, built on it, could disclose. [15]

And now he could be called the "friend of God," not only by God Himself, but also by men (cf. Isa. 41:8; 2 Chr. 20:7). This is in fact the name by which Abraham has been known down through the centuries in many lands and by at least three religions (Christianity, Judaism, Islam). Had Abraham not obeyed God in the greatest test of his life, he would still have been justified by the faith he exercised in Genesis 15:6. But by allowing that faith to be *alive* in his works, he attained an enviable title among men. In this way he was also justified by works!

When a man is justified by faith he finds an unqualified acceptance before God. As Paul puts it, such a man is one "to whom God imputes righteousness without works" (Rom. 4:6). But only God can see this spiritual transaction. When, however, a man is justified by works he achieves an intimacy with God that is manifest to men. He can then be called "the friend of God," even as Jesus said, "You are My friends if you do whatever I command you" (John 15:14).[16]

(7) James's Concluding Words (2:24-26)

Leaving the imagined objector behind, James returns in verses 24-26 to address the readership directly. Rahab furnishes him with his final Biblical example of justification by works. James says:

> You see then that a man is justified by works, and not by faith only. Likewise, was not Rahab the harlot justified by works when she received the messengers and sent them out another way? For as the body without the spirit is dead, so faith without works is dead also (Jam. 2:24-26).

It should be carefully observed that he does *not* say, "Was not Rahab justified by faith *and* works"! As already mentioned, such an idea is foreign to James. He is talking about exactly what he says he is talking about: justification by works!

Rahab, however, is superbly suited to tie his thoughts together. The passage had begun, as we have seen, with a reference to his theme of "saving the life" (2:14; 1:21). Not surprisingly, Rahab is selected as a striking example of a person whose physical life was "saved" precisely because she had works.

With James's words the statement of the writer of Hebrews can be profitably compared. In 11:31, that author writes of her:

> By faith the harlot Rahab did not perish with
> those who did not believe, when she had
> received the spies with peace.

Notice that the author of Hebrews points to her faith and lays the stress on the fact that she "received" the spies. James, on the other hand, points also to the fact that "she sent them out another way." This has considerable significance for James's argument.

Although Rahab's faith began to operate the moment she "received the messengers," she could not really be justified by works until she had "sent them out another way." The reason for this is obvious when the story in Joshua 2 is carefully considered. Up until the last moment, she could still have betrayed the spies. Had she so desired, she could have sent their pursuers after them.

That the spies had lingering doubts about her loyalty is suggested by their words in Joshua 2:20, "And if you tell this business of ours, then we will be free from your oath . . . " But the spies' successful escape demonstrated that Rahab was truly a "friend of God" because she was also *their* friend. In this way, Rahab was justified by works. [17]

And in the process, she saved her own life and her family's! Her faith, therefore, was very much *alive* because it was an active, working faith. Though she was a harlot - and both inspired writers remind us that she was - her living faith triumphed over the natural consequences of her sin. While all the inhabitants of

Jericho perished under the divine judgment which Israel executed, she *lived* because her faith *lived!*

James therefore wishes his readers to know that works are in fact the vitalizing "spirit" which keeps one's faith alive in the same way that the human spirit keeps the human body alive (2:26). Whenever a Christian ceases to act on his faith, that faith atrophies and becomes little more than a creedal corpse. "Dead orthodoxy" is a danger that has always confronted Christian people and they do well to take heed to this danger.[18] But the antidote is a simple one: faith remains vital and alive as long as it is being translated into real works of living obedience.

Summary

Does James contradict Paul's doctrine of free grace, or John's insistence on faith as the single condition of eternal life? Far from it. But neither does he offer support to the widespread notion that a "dead faith" cannot exist in the life of a Christian. Ironically, that is exactly what he is warning against. Thus, a misunderstanding of his words has not only promoted confusion about the terms for eternal life, but it has also deprived the Church of a much-needed warning.[19]

The dangers of a dead faith are real. But these dangers do not include hell.[20] Nothing James writes suggests this. Nevertheless, sin remains a deadly enemy to Christian experience which can prematurely end our physical lives. The wisdom of the Old Testament and James are agreed about this. So, if Christians are to be "saved" from that result, they will need more than faith.

They will also need works.[21]

CHAPTER

4

LUKE 14:
THE COST OF DISCIPLESHIP

One fact which the Lord Jesus Christ made completely clear was that discipleship involved a costly commitment. On that point His words left no doubt.

A classic expression of this truth is found in Luke 14:26, 27. There the Savior declares:

> "If anyone comes to Me and does not hate his father and mother, wife and children, brothers and sisters, yes, and his own life also, he cannot be My disciple. And whoever does not bear his cross and come after Me cannot be My disciple."

Later, in the same context (14:33), He says:

> "So likewise, whoever of you does not forsake all that he has, he cannot be My disciple."

It is part of the contemporary siege of the Gospel that such words are often taken today as expressing virtual conditions for eternal salvation. The word "virtual" is deliberately chosen. It is often claimed that those who do not fulfill the terms of discipleship will not go to heaven. Yet at the same time those who say this might insist on Paul's doctrine that a man is saved by grace through faith and apart from works. The inconsistency of this is glaring.

In response to this charge, some indeed would claim that discipleship is *not* a condition for eternal life, but an *inevitable result* of possessing it. But those who so speak are playing a word-game. Whatever is *necessary* to achieve a goal is also a *condition* for reaching it. To call anything an *inevitable* result is to call it a *necessary* result and thus to make it a *condition*. Candor is lacking in those who fail to admit this. [1]

Let's put it plainly. If on-going good works are necessary for reaching heaven, they are also a *condition* for reaching heaven. Thus, on this view, final salvation is based on faith *plus* works! But how few are the theologians who will clearly admit this! The present debate suffers from a shortage of theological honesty.

Looking at Luke 14

By no stretch of the imagination can the words of Jesus in Luke 14 be treated as portraying the "inevitable result" of regeneration. There is absolutely nothing in the passage to suggest that. On the contrary, the obvious purpose of the Lord's statements is to warn against the very real danger of failure.

The well-known image of the man and the uncompleted tower serves to highlight this aspect of the passage (Luke 14:28-30). The words with which he is mocked carry a pointed message: "This man began to build and was not able to finish." In the same way, the metaphor of the king who sues for peace carries a similar warning (Luke 14:31-32). Discipleship, Jesus warns, can end in failure.

If the claim is advanced that no real Christian is subject to such failure, that claim amounts to little more than an evasion of the warning itself. Certainly there is nothing in the Biblical text to suggest this point of view. To invoke it is to read something *into* the text that cannot be supported or verified.

The issue can be simply put: Can a man who trusts Christ for eternal life but fails to "hate" his father and mother go to heaven (Luke 14:26)? If the answer to this is "no," then it is perfectly clear that "hating" one's father and mother is a *condition* for final salvation. No amount of theological re-articulation can conceal this result. But in the process, the terms of the Biblical Gospel have been radically transformed. Heaven cannot be reached except by the most strenuous self-denial and loyalty to Christ. Salvation by grace through faith alone becomes a mere fiction or a theological illusion.

How serious this is can hardly be overstated. Those who express their conception of the Gospel of Christ this way must necessarily feel restless and uncomfortable in the presence of our Lord's free and unencumbered offer to the sinful woman of Sychar. Had she been told the stringent demands of Luke 14, she could scarcely have imagined that she was being offered a *gift!* For that matter, who could?

It is an interpretative mistake of the first magnitude to confuse the terms of discipleship with the offer of eternal life as a free gift. "And whoever desires, let him take the water of life freely" (Rev. 22:17), is clearly an unconditional offer.[2] "If any one comes to Me and does not . . . he cannot be My disciple" clearly expresses a relationship which is fully conditional. Not to recognize this simple distinction is to invite confusion and error at the most fundamental level.

Looking at John 8

The distinction between salvation and discipleship is openly recognized in the Gospel of John. In John 8:30 we are told, "As He spoke these words, many believed in Him." In the original Greek the words "believed in Him" represent a special phrase which is almost (though not quite) unique to the Fourth Gospel. This phrase involves the use of a Greek preposition (*eis*) after the verb for "believe" and, so far at least, it has not been found in secular Greek. Among the instances of its use in John's Gospel may be mentioned the following: 1:12; 2:11; 3:15,

16, 18, 36; 6:29, 35, 40, 47; 7:38, 39; 9:35, 36; 10:42; 11:25, 26, 45; and 12:44, 46.

Even a rapid examination of these texts shows that this specialized expression is John's standard way of describing the act of saving faith by which eternal life is obtained. To deny this in John 8:30 would be to go directly counter to the well-established usage of the author. Yet precisely to these individuals who had exercised saving faith, Jesus adds:

> "If you abide in My word, you are My disciples indeed. And you shall know the truth, and the truth shall make you free" (8:31, 32).

On the authority of Jesus Himself it can be said that the believers of John 8:30 received eternal life in response to their faith. It was He who had affirmed, "Most assuredly, I say to you, he who believes in Me has everlasting life" (John 6:47). But to these who now had that life, Jesus set forth a *conditional* relationship: "*If* you abide in My word, you are My disciples indeed."

Plainly we have here, as also in Luke 14, a relationship which depends on the individual's continuing commitment to the discipleship experience. Should this commitment fail, he would become like the man who "began to build and was not able to finish." But this reality should not be confused with a man's permanent possession of the gift of eternal life. That gift, like all God's gifts, is irrevocable (Rom. 11:29). The one who acquires it can never hunger or thirst for it again (John 6:35). Moreover, the Lord Jesus Christ will never lose anyone who has trusted Him for it (John 6:37-40).

Despite what has just been said, it has actually been argued that the individuals of John 8:30 exercised a faith that was not regenerating. An appeal is sometimes made to the Greek phrase in verse 31, "the Jews who believed Him." Here it is said that John uses an expression without the preposition (that is, without the *eis* found in verse 30) and that this signals the inadequacy of the faith which these Jews had.

This argument is groundless. John knows nothing about a faith in Christ that is not saving. The construction found in verse 31 appears also in John 5:24 where no one would regard it as expressing faulty belief. It is equally obvious that the individuals of verse 31 are the same as those of verse 30 where John employs his specialized expression. The effort to distinguish different *kinds* of faith, both here and elsewhere, is entirely futile.[3] (John 2:23 and 12:42 are sometimes suggested, but on question-begging grounds. In both cases, genuine salvation occurs since John's single condition of faith is met.)[4]

It has also been claimed, however, that the believing Jews of verses 30, 31 are the speakers in verses 33, 39 and 41. It is then pointed out that in verse 44 Jesus tells them, "You are of your father the devil, and the desires of your father you want to do." Along with the whole tenor of verses 33-47 (and especially the statements of verses 39, 40 and 42) this is seen as a clear indication that the faith described in 8:30 was not regenerating faith.

But this argument involves a misassessment of the whole context in which verses 8:30-32 are placed.

John 8:13-59 is clearly a controversy section which has its setting in the Jewish Temple (8:20). Jesus' opponents throughout the section are His general audience in the Temple treasury. They are described as Pharisees (8:13), as Jews (8:22, 48, 52 and 57), and more simply as "they" (8:19, 25, 27, 33, 39, 41, 59). John does not expect us to understand the "they" of verse 33 any differently than we do the same word in verses 19, 25, and 27. He means the larger audience.[5]

Verses 30, 31a (about those who believe in Him) are a kind of "aside" to the reader to explain the background and purpose of Jesus' statement in verses 31b, 32 (about continuing in His Word). In this way the reader is allowed to learn the reason why Jesus' words are misunderstood and how they serve to intensify the controversy that is already raging.

This technique is thoroughly Johannine. Throughout the Fourth Gospel, the words of Jesus are frequently misunderstood (cf. 3:4; 4:11, 12; 6:34; 7:35; 8:22; etc.). Where necessary, John offers the readers the crucial clue to their actual meaning (cf. 2:19-22; 11:11-13). This is what he is doing in verses 30-31a. The reader is "tipped off" about the real purpose behind the words in 3:31b-32.

Thus there is no reason at all to suppose that when John states that "many believed in Him" (8:30) he means anything different than he does with nearly identical statements in 10:42 and 11:45. The effort to see the "believers" of 8:30, 31 as belonging to some special category (like an "unregenerate believer"!) is without foundation and is totally misguided.

John 8:30-32 can stand therefore as a significant contribution to our understanding of the difference between the terms of discipleship and the condition for receiving eternal life. The latter here, as everywhere in the Fourth Gospel, is the result of faith. But discipleship depends upon the believer's continuance in the Word of Christ. This is plain enough and should occasion no confusion at all.

Disciples Are Pupils

Of course, the Greek word for "disciple" meant simply a "pupil" or a "learner." Thus a disciple was one who was "in school" – that is, he was under the guidance and instruction of a teacher.

In the Greco-Roman world of New Testament times there were many traveling teachers. Experts in such fields as philosophy or rhetoric traveled from place to place and taught their specialty. Jewish rabbis often did the same. The idea of a pupil, or disciple, leaving home to follow such a teacher around and learn from him, was not a strange idea at all.

The cultural gap between ourselves and the first century has probably contributed to the modern confusion about discipleship. No doubt close attention to the Scriptures could have spared us from that. But it is important to see things like this in their historical setting.

In the first century, no one would be surprised if someone who had left home to follow a traveling teacher were tempted to "drop out" and return to his loved ones. In this light, continuing commitment to Christ and His Word, even above commitment to the family itself, is a natural condition for the kind of relationship which discipleship describes. By contrast, regeneration points to a family relationship in which God becomes the Father of the one who trusts His Son. Such relationships on earth are permanent. The divine family is no exception.

It is not surprising that in the Book of Acts the word "disciple" becomes a standard way of describing those who became a part of the visible church. The "school" in which they now received their instruction was the church itself. It was there that the doctrine of the Apostles brought them into vital contact with all that Jesus Himself had taught these original disciples.

It was in the church, then, that the first disciples reproduced themselves by making other disciples. The steps involved in this process were twofold, as Matthew 28:19, 20 disclose:

> "Go therefore and make disciples of all the nations, **baptizing** them in the name of the Father and of the Son and of the Holy Spirit, **teaching** them to observe all things that I have commanded you; and lo, I am with you always, even to the end of the age" (emphasis added).

The process of disciple-making involves, therefore, an initiation (baptizing) followed by indoctrination (teaching). Both steps were begun promptly on the first day of the Church's history, immediately after the conversion of three thousand souls (Acts 2:41, 42).

It should be noticed that from the beginning baptism was associated with the making of disciples. John notes that "the Pharisees had heard that Jesus made and baptized more disciples than John (though Jesus Himself did not baptize, but His disciples)" (John 4:1, 2). Baptism can properly be seen as the first concrete step which a disciple takes in obedience to Christ.

A Disciple "Abides"

It is of considerable interest that the word used by our Lord in John 8:31 to describe the responsibility of a disciple is an important one in the Fourth Gospel. The word "abide" is exactly the same word that is also translated "abide" in John 15:1-7. There it is the crucial term in the metaphor about the vine and its branches.

Of course, the same word can be used of the mutually shared life of the believer and Christ (John 6:56) as well as of a purely physical dwelling (= "staying," John 1:38, 39). But in John 15 its role in the metaphor is evidently to describe the discipleship experience.

This observation is supported by the text. The discussion of the vine and branches is concluded in 15:8 with the words:

> "By this My Father is glorified, that you bear
> much fruit; so *you will be My disciples*"
> (emphasis added).

A recognition that this famous passage applies to discipleship dissolves the problems which have often been associated with it.

As already observed, discipleship is a conditional relationship that can be interrupted or terminated after it has begun. This obviously is also true of the vine/branch relationship described in John 15. It is the responsibility of Jesus' disciples (to whom these words are spoken) to "abide" in Him (15:4). When this condition is fulfilled, there is fruitfulness (15:5) and answered prayer (15:7). If the condition is *not* fulfilled, tragic consequences occur (15:6).

"Abiding," we may say, is based on learning and keeping the commands of our Teacher. When we live disobediently, we are not abiding (see 1 John 2:5, 6).

The consequences that follow when a disciple fails to abide in Christ (John 15:6) are very meaningful in terms of the Teacher/pupil relationship. First, there is the loss of the relationship itself: "he is cast out as a branch." Next, there is the loss of the spiritual vitality associated with that relationship: "and is withered." Finally, there is chastening: "they gather them and throw them into the fire, and they are burned."

It is entirely unnecessary to associate the "fire" of John 15:6 with the literal fires of hell. After all, the entire passage involves a figure of speech. The "vine" is not a literal vine, the "branches" are not literal branches, nor the "fruit" literal fruit. There is no reason either why the "fire" must be literal fire. Instead it serves as an effective metaphor for whatever trials or hardships may attend the life of a lapsed disciple. "Fire" as a figure for temporal afflictions is a commonplace in the Bible and, indeed, in all of literature (see Deut. 32:22-24; Ps. 78:21; Isa. 9:18, 19; Jer. 15:14; Amos 1:4, 7, 10, 12; etc.)

Whether restoration of a branch to its former position in the vine is possible or not is a point that lies outside the scope of the metaphor. But it can be noticed that the process of withering suggests a lapse of time prior to the experience of the fire itself. What is not possible in nature, of course, is possible with God. It is unwise to push a figure of speech too far or to require it to express ideas which it is not capable of bearing. It is sufficient to learn from our Lord's words that abiding is crucial to fruitfulness and that the failure to abide can lead to spiritual disaster.

Much perplexity has been created by expositions of John 15 which identified John's ideas with Paul's concept that believers are "in Christ" (e.g., Eph. 1:3). But this identification is superficial and unwarranted. The conditional character of the abiding relationship should have told us that from the beginning.

John 10:27, 28 and Discipleship

It is extremely dangerous in the interpretation of Scripture to equate unthinkingly the meanings of words and expressions that are found in widely differing contexts. The equation of the "in Me" of John 15 with Paul's "in Christ" is only one case in point. Another which affects the present discussion on discipleship involves John 10:27, 28.

In those verses Jesus affirms:

> "My sheep hear My voice, and I know them,
> and they follow Me. And I give them eternal
> life, and they shall never perish; neither shall
> anyone snatch them out of My hand."

It has been quite common to identify the term "follow" in these verses with the experience of discipleship, in which men are challenged to follow Christ. But again the identification cannot withstand examination.

Those who hold that the word "follow" in John 10:27 must mean something like "obey" have rarely stopped to ask a very relevant question. What accounts for the sequence here? Why does Jesus say, "They follow Me and I give them eternal life," rather than, "I give them eternal life and they follow Me"? It sounds as though the giving of eternal life is *the result of* His sheep following Him. As a matter of fact, this conclusion is undoubtedly correct!

A comparison of John 10:27, 28 with John 5:24 will show how natural this conclusion is within the familiar context of John's thought. John 5:24 contains several distinct elements: (1) the hearing of Christ's word; (2) faith; (3) the possession of eternal life; (4) a guarantee against judgment; (5) a secure situation ("passed from death into life").

All of these elements are echoed in John 10:27, 28. The only new feature is the expression, "I know them," which is contextually determined by the stress on Jesus' capacity to recognize His own sheep (10:14, 26). Leaving this aside, we have the following features in verses 27 and 28: (1) hearing Christ's voice; (2) following; (3) the giving of eternal life; (4) a guarantee against perishing; (5) a secure situation (in Jesus' hand).

This leads readily to the conclusion that in John 10:27 the term "follow" is simply another Johannine metaphor for saving faith.   Like the metaphors about receiving (1:12), drinking (4:14), coming (6:35, 37), eating bread (6:35), eating Christ's flesh and drinking His blood (6:54) and others, "follow" expresses the action in response to which eternal life is bestowed.   When the Shepherd calls the sheep through His Word (and He knows who they are), they respond to that call by following Him.   That is to say, they commit their safety and well-being to the Shepherd who has summoned them to do so.   A sheep's instinctive fear of strange voices lies in the background of this analogy (see 10:4, 5), so that the decision to follow is after all an act of *trust.*

It is a mistake to understand the word "follow" in John 10:27 as though it indicates something about the nature of the believer's experience *after* he receives eternal life.   In fact it has nothing to do with that at all, as its position in our Lord's statements enables us to see.

In the final analysis, John 10:27, 28 merely expresses in a fresh way the truth presented in John 5:24.   The *immediately preceding* verses in John 10 show that the fundamental issue in Jesus' exchange with the Jews is *faith.*   Thus in verses 25 and 26 Jesus tells them:

> "I told you, and you do not **believe**. The works that I do in My Father's name, they bear witness of Me.   But you do not **believe**, because you are not of My sheep, as I said to you" (emphasis added).

When John 10:27 is read in connection with these statements, its meaning is clear.   These Jews are not His sheep because they do not *believe*, but His real sheep *follow*, i.e., they *believe*!   Hence, John 10:27 and 28 have nothing to do with the subject of discipleship.[6]

Conclusion

Expositors of God's Word are under a solemn responsibility to pay close attention to the exact nature of Scriptural declarations.   The failure to do this is a primary reason why the theme of discipleship has often been confused with the Gospel of God's free saving grace. This confusion in turn has played into the hands of the Enemy with a resulting distortion of the terms on which man may obtain a place in heaven.   It is high time for the Christian Church to renounce the theological errors that result from this and to reaffirm its commitment to the gift of God.

Only then can we be completely honest about the costs and dangers of true discipleship.

CHAPTER

5

1 JOHN:
TESTS OF LIFE?

The Epistle of 1 John is the work of the same inspired writer who penned the Gospel of John. It is ironic that in the modern church it is often used in a way that is incompatible with the free offer of life found in the Fourth Gospel.

One well-known view of the purpose of 1 John maintains that the epistle offers us "tests of life."[1] That is, John confronts his readership with questions about the quality of their Christian experience from which they may draw the conclusion that they either are, or are not, true believers. Should they fail to measure up, they have no reason to think that they possess eternal life.

It would be hard to devise an approach to John's first epistle more hopelessly misguided or more completely self-defeating. If the premise on which this approach is based were true, it would be quite impossible for either the original audience of 1 John or any of its subsequent readers to possess the assurance of salvation.

Since the writer repeatedly commands the "abiding" life marked by obedience to Christ's commands, one cannot really be certain that he is saved until death, if "abiding" is a test of salvation. On the view we are discussing, if I stop "abiding" at some point in the future, I was never a Christian at all.

This view is absurd in the light of the NT. Basically it denies the vibrant confidence in our relationship to God which the NT everywhere teaches us to have. In its place it puts a gnawing doubt that my whole "Christian experience" may prove in the end to have been an illusion.

The Readers of 1 John are Saved

Few errors of contemporary Bible exposition are more blatant than the one we have mentioned. Not only does John not say that he is writing to "test" whether his readers are saved or not, he says the reverse! This is amply proved from a notable passage in the second chapter:

> I write to you, little children, because *your sins are forgiven* you for His name's sake. I write to you, fathers, because you have known Him who is from the beginning. I write to you, young men, because you have overcome the wicked one. I write to you, little children, because *you have known the Father.* I have written to you, fathers, because you have known Him who is from the beginning. I have written to you, young men, because you are strong, and the word of God abides in you, and you have overcome the wicked one (1 John 2:12-14; emphasis added).

So far from writing to his readers because he, or they, need to "test" the reality of their Christian experience, John writes precisely because that experience is real!

It should be carefully noted that the passage quoted above is immediately followed by a solemn warning:

> Do not love the world or the things in the world. If anyone loves the world, the love of the Father is not in him. For all that is in the world – the lust of the flesh, the lust of the

eyes, and the pride of life – is not of the
Father but is of the world (2:15, 16).

Coming as this warning does directly after the reassuring
words of 2:12-14, the exhortation tells us a great deal. It
reveals that from John's point of view morality can be
effectively produced in people who are sure about their
relationship to God. Morality is not the grounds for
assurance, but the fruit of it.

Paul also believed the same thing. He can therefore
exhort the Ephesian Christians "to walk worthy of the
calling with which you were called" (Eph. 4:1). Or he can
say, "Therefore, as the elect of God, holy and beloved, put
on tender mercies, kindness, humility, meekness,
longsuffering" (Col. 3:12). He can also add, "forgiving one
another . . . even as Christ forgave you, so you also must
do" (Col. 3:13). In 1 Corinthians 6:15-20, he even bases his
appeal to avoid immorality on what his readers should
know. Their body is the Spirit's temple (vs. 19); they
belong to God in both body and spirit (vs. 20). *Therefore,*
they should flee sexual sin!

It is a serious misconception to think that godly living
is undermined if believers know already that they belong
to Christ forever. On the contrary, the joy and gratitude of
an assured relationship to God are precisely the well-
springs from which holiness most naturally arises. The
New Testament writers, at least, believed this strongly,
even if we do not. The writer of 1 John believed it
emphatically.

John's Realism About
Possible Failure

The appeal which John makes (2:15-17) to avoid the
enticements of the world demonstrates also his practical
realism. He knows full well that the world possesses a
deceptive attractiveness to which even true Christians
may fall prey.

In particular, in this epistle, he is concerned with the

worldly point of view put forth by the false teachers against whom he writes. These antichrists, as he fittingly calls them (2:18, 22), "are of the world. Therefore they speak as of the world, and the world hears them" (4:5). The readers need to be reminded of their true relationship to Christ so that they may effectively resist the false ideas to which they are being exposed.

One idea that the antichrists may have advanced was that the readers were not after all genuinely saved. It seems possible that the false teachers were the forerunners of the later gnostic heretics, and if so, this is very likely to have been one of their opinions. A strong streak of elitism ran through gnostic thought. The gnostics alone could look forward to eternal happiness or bliss (however they may have defined this). The antichrists may have suggested that the readers did not have eternal life at all, and that they needed to adopt the "gnosis" (knowledge), which the gnostics brought, in order to have it.[2]

That something like this was indeed part of the problem is strongly hinted at toward the end of John's first critique of the antichrists. This critique, which begins in 2:18, reaches its climax in 2:25-27.

It is in verse 25 that John reminds his readers:

> And this is the promise that He has promised us – eternal life.

Having said this, he adds at once,

> These things I have written to you concerning those who try to deceive you (2:26).

The close connection of these two statements certainly makes it probable that the false teachers denied the divine promise about eternal life on which the readers were relying.

The readers, therefore, must be assured that "I have not written to you because you do not know the truth, but because you know it, and that no lie is of the truth" (2:21). Their responsibility is to "let that abide in you which you heard from the beginning" (2:24a). They are not to give way before the falsehoods they are now hearing. And if they do hold on to the Christian truth they already know, the abiding life will be their continuing experience. "If what you heard from the beginning abides in you, you also will abide in the Son and in the Father" (2:24b).

But here, as we have already seen in John 8 and John 15, the abiding life is a conditional experience. The words, "*If* what you have heard from the beginning abides in you," show this. John is perfectly sure that his readers are forgiven, know God, have experienced victory over the wicked one and know the truth, because he says so (2:12-14, 21). But he is *not* equally sure that the readership will not be seduced by the worldly spirit which they are now confronting.

This perspective is precisely the opposite of the view that is so frequently taken of John's first epistle. So far from commanding his readers to "abide" in order to assure themselves that they are truly saved, he in fact assures them they are saved and challenges them on that basis to abide. How do they know they are saved? They have the divine promise of eternal life (2:25)!

The Purpose of 1 John: Fellowship

If all of this is kept in mind, the reader of 1 John will be able to grasp the meaning of the important statement found in 5:13. There the Apostle declares,

> These things I have written to you who believe in the name of the Son of God, that you may know that you have eternal life.

This statement is frequently and wrongly taken as a statement of purpose for the entire epistle. It assumes mistakenly that the expression "these things" refers to the letter as a whole.[3]   But this is contrary to the writer's usage. In 2:1, the words "these things I write" clearly refer to the immediately preceding discussion of sin in 1:5-10. In 2:26, a comparable statement refers with equal clarity to the previous section about the antichrists. From these two earlier examples, we would naturally draw the conclusion that the "these things" of 5:13 is most likely to refer to the subject matter right before it.

This conclusion is fully justified by the content of 1 John 5:9-12. In fact, in these verses alone do we find in this epistle a direct discussion of faith and eternal life. The passage deserves quotation:

> If we receive the witness of men, the witness of God is greater; for this is the witness of God which He has testified of His Son. He who believes in the Son of God has the witness in himself; he who does not believe God has made Him a liar, because he has not believed the testimony that God has given of His Son. And this is the testimony: that God has given us eternal life, and this life is in His Son. He who has the Son has life; he who does not have the Son of God does not have life (1 John 5:9-12).

It is to these statements that John adds in verse 13,

> These things I have written to you who believe in the name of the Son of God, *that you may know* that you have eternal life (emphasis added).

In a passage like this we are plainly breathing once again the atmosphere of the Fourth Gospel and of verses like John 5:24. There is nothing in 1 John 5:9-12 about "obedience" or "abiding" or anything else of that sort. Everything is made to hinge on whether or not we can accept God's testimony about His Son.

Moreover, eternal life is seen as something God "has

given" us in His Son – that is, as always for John, it is a divine gift. It is precisely these reaffirmations of the simple Gospel that are the grounds on which the Apostle expects his readers to *know* that they possess eternal life. To put it simply, they are to trust "the promise that He has promised" them (2:25).

There is no reason, therefore, to seek the purpose of this epistle exclusively in 1 John 5:13 anymore than it is to be sought exclusively in 2:1 or 2:26. Instead, the most natural place to look for the overarching thrust of the the letter is in its prologue. *And there the purpose is defined clearly as "fellowship" with God.*

John introduces his epistle like this:

> That which was from the beginning, which we have heard, which we have seen with our eyes, which we have looked upon, and our hands have handled, concerning the Word of life . . . that which we have seen and heard we declare to you, that you also may have fellowship with us; and truly our fellowship is with the Father and with His Son Jesus Christ (1:1, 3).

Much confusion could have been avoided in the study of John's epistle if this initial declaration of intent had been clearly kept in mind. Fellowship is John's primary concern and goal.[4]

The Threat to Fellowship

It should go without saying that "fellowship" is not to be defined as practically a synonym for being a Christian.[5] King David was surely a regenerate man when he committed adultery and murder, but he could not be said to have been in God's fellowship at the time!

Even on a human plane, a son or daughter may lose fellowship with a parent even though they do not thereby lose the family relationship. The equation of "fellowship" with "being a Christian" (or something similar) is extremely far-fetched. Fellowship, like abiding, is a fully conditional relationship.   This fact is sufficiently demonstrated by the statements found in 1:5-10.

Fellowship was precisely what was threatened by the false ideas of the antichrists. Since the readers had a divine promise about eternal life, nothing these false prophets could do or say could destroy the readers' fundamental relationship to God.   But should the readership begin to listen to the doctrines of these men, their experience of fellowship with the Father and the Son would be in jeopardy.   Up to now, the readers had apparently resisted the false teaching successfully (4:4). The Apostle wishes this resistance to continue (2:24-27).

Ironically, the antichrists with whom John is concerned had evidently arisen right out of the Apostolic circle itself.   This is indicated by the statement in 2:19 which says:

> They went out from us, but they were not of us; for if they had been of us, they would have continued with us; but they went out that they might be made manifest, that none of them were of us.

In this interesting statement, the word "us" indicates the apostolic circle to which the writer belongs.   This is shown by the immediate contrast with "you" found in verse 20.   This we/you contrast appears for the first time in the prologue itself (1:1-3) and again, clearly, in 4:4-6.   In the latter passage the "they" (4:5) refers to the antichrists, as it also does here in 2:19.

The false prophets had therefore withdrawn from the apostolic fellowship, which probably means that they had once been a part of the Palestinian church. Jerusalem and Judea had long been the orbit of direct apostolic influence and authority.   But roots like this could give their teachings an aura of respectability which might have a dangerous impact on the readership to whom they had come.

In this respect, these people had something in common with the legalists of Acts 15:1, since the legalists also came to Antioch from Judea. The Jerusalem Council denied any connection with them (15:24) just as John does here.

The statement of 2:19 cannot be taken as a general proposition about the lifestyle of the born-again believer. John is talking about heresy and defection from the faith and declaring that such defection would have been inconceivable if these individuals had truly shared the Apostles' spirit and perspective.

His words bear a striking resemblance to the observation of the Apostle Paul in 1 Corinthians 11:18, 19:

> For first of all, when you come together as a church, I hear that there are divisions among you, and in part I believe it. For there must also be factions among you, that those who are approved may be recognized among you.

Paul's comment is instructive. Heresy and division, even among genuine Christians (he does *not* suggest that any of his readers are *not* Christians), is designed by God to distinguish those who merit His approval from those who do not. Heresy does not occur in a vacuum. Rather it unmasks deep spiritual deficiencies which otherwise might go undetected.

This is essentially what John declares here as well. The withdrawal of these false teachers unmasked their fundamental disharmony with the outlook of the Apostles. In that sense "they were not of us."[6]

To say more than this is to go beyond the text. No doubt the antichrists *were* unsaved. But this is not the point. Even if they *had been* genuine believers, such a withdrawing could not have taken place if – and as long as – they truly shared the apostolic spirit and commitment to the truth. To make a general expression like "of us" mean something more specific than that is not warranted in any way.

The principal source of confusion in much contemporary study of 1 John is to be found in the failure to recognize the real danger against which the writer is warning. The eternal salvation of the readership is not imperiled. It is not even in doubt as far as the author is concerned.

But seduction by the world and its antichristian representatives was a genuine threat which had to be faced. Along with their heretical denials of the Person of Christ (2:22, 23; 4:1-3), the false teachers evidently also promoted a lifestyle that was basically worldly and unloving. If the readers went in *that* direction, they would lose fellowship both with the Apostles themselves as well as with the Father and the Son (see 1:3).

Fellowship and the Knowledge of God

It is certainly not by chance that a general warning against the selfish and lustful spirit of the world (2:15-17) immediately precedes the first specific warning against the antichrists (2:18-27). Again, the second direct caution against false prophets (4:1-6) is followed by an exhortation to "love one another" (4:7) and an extended passage on love (4:7-21). If the readers should begin to doubt the reality of their personal salvation and their fundamental relationship to God, they would be more easily enticed into the loveless, self-seeking lifestyle all around them.

The readers need to know, therefore, that they truly have eternal life (2:25; 5:13) and are called to experience fellowship with the Apostles themselves (1:3a) and with the Father and the Son (1:3b). To surrender such fellowship (they apparently had not done so yet) would be to surrender the privilege of truly *knowing God.*

In ordinary human life, fellowship with an individual is the essential means for gaining an intimate knowledge of that individual. Friends come to know friends, and even children come to know their parents, by means of shared time and experience – that is, through "fellowship."

The same is true also at the level of our relationship to God. While in one sense all true Christians know God (John 17:3), it is possible to think of a sense in which a true Christian may *not* know God.

This is made clear in a striking remark by the Lord Jesus Christ in John 14:7. There he declares to His disciples:

> "If you had known Me, you would have known My Father also; and from now on you know Him and have seen Him."

The form of the conditional sentence in Greek indicates (as the English does also) that up to this moment the disciples had, in a special sense, not really known Jesus or His Father.[7] When Philip at once requests to see the Father (14:8), his ignorance about Christ is reaffirmed:

> Jesus said to him, "Have I been with you so long, and yet you have not known Me, Philip? He who has seen Me has seen the Father; so how can you say, 'Show us the Father'?" (14:9).

Despite the fact that Philip and the other disciples had believed in Jesus (John 1:40-51; 2:11) and had eternal life, the Person of their Savior remained something of a mystery to them. They had not yet realized how fully He reflected His Father (14:10) and, in this sense, they did not *know* Him!

Later in the same chapter Jesus offers a personal self-disclosure to His disciples which is conditioned on their obedience to His commands. His statement shows that He speaks of a future experience for them which will involve intimacy with Himself and His Father. His words are given in John 14:21-24:

> "He who has My commandments and keeps

> them, it is he who loves Me. And he who
> loves Me will be loved by My Father, and I will
> love him and **manifest Myself** to him."
> Judas (not Iscariot) said to Him, "Lord, how is
> it that you **will manifest Yourself** to us,
> and not to the world?" Jesus answered and
> said to him, "If anyone loves Me, he will keep
> My Word; and My Father will love him, and
> We will come to him and **make Our home**
> with him. He who does not love Me does not
> keep My words; and the word which you
> hear is not Mine but the Father's who sent
> Me" (emphasis added).

It is plain from this passage that "fellowship" and "the knowledge of God" are implied in the offer Jesus is making. Even the concept of the "abiding" life is suggested by the Greek word for "home" which is related to the word for "abide." But everything depends on the love that the disciples have for their Lord, which is seen as the true source of obedience to His commands.

It is precisely this kind of truth that pervades John's first epistle. "Fellowship" is its overriding theme. This means quite simply the "abiding" life marked by the self-disclosure of Christ, that is, by the knowledge of God.

But just as in John 14:21-24, such an experience can only be claimed by those who obey Jesus' commandments (1 John 2:3-6). The readers need to keep this in mind with regard to any false claims to "knowledge" which they may have heard. And they need to apply it to their own personal lives.

Particularly striking in regard to the theme of "knowing God" is the statement made in 1 John 4:7, 8:

> Beloved, let us love one another, for love is
> of God; and everyone who loves is born of
> God and knows God. He who does not love
> does not know God, for God is love.

It would be natural to conclude from this text that "new

birth" and "knowing God" can be distinguished. If a man loves (in the Christian sense of that word), both experiences can be predicated of him. If he does *not* love, all that John states is that he does not *know* God. John does not say, however, that he is not *born* of God![8]

It would have been easy for the Apostle to have said this if he had believed it. But when it comes to failure in Christian experience, *including the failure to love*, John is a hardheaded realist. He is, in fact, much more of a realist than are many modern theologians.

Sin in the Christian's Life

John's realism extends to his discussion about sin in the believer's life.

According to John, there is no time when a Christian may say he is sinless. Indeed, "If we say that we have no sin, we deceive ourselves, and the truth is not in us" (1 John 1:8). One indication that the truth has an effective hold on the Christian's heart is his awareness that he is a sinful person. Of course, this must be accompanied by a willingness to confess his sin whenever he detects it (1:9). Not to do so is to hide from reality and to live in the dark (cf. 1:5-7).

There is no fellowship with God in the dark.

Some have thought, however, that John contradicts his earlier insistence on the reality of sin in a Christian's life by his later words in 3:6 and 9. In those places, the Apostle writes:

> Whoever abides in him does not sin. Whoever sins has neither seen Him nor known Him (3:6).
> Whoever has been born of God does not sin, for His seed remains in him; and he cannot sin, because he has been born of God (3:9).

These statements are straightforward enough and ought

not to be watered down or explained away. Nevertheless, they do not contradict 1:8.

In modern times a popular method for dealing with the problems of 1 John 3:6, 9 has been to appeal to the use of the Greek present tense. It is claimed that this tense requires a translation like, "Whoever has been born of God does not *go on* sinning," or, "does not *continually* sin." The conclusion to be drawn from such renderings is that, though the Christian may sin somewhat (how much is never specified!), he may not sin regularly or persistently. But on all grounds, whether linguistic or exegetical, this approach is indefensible.

The appeal to the present tense has long invited suspicion.[9] No other text can be cited where the Greek present tense, unaided by qualifying words, can carry this kind of significance. Indeed, when the Greek writer or speaker wished to indicate that an action was, or was not, continual, there were special words to express this.[10]

But this is not all. The "tense solution" lands its proponents in enormous difficulties and inconsistencies. Thus, in 1:8, if the present tense were read in this way, we would have the following: "If we say we do not *continually* have sin, we deceive ourselves and the truth is not in us." But if the tense explanation for 3:9 were correct, we ought to be able to say this. It should not be self-deception to make this claim if "whoever is born of God does not *continually* sin"![11]

In the same way, if the tense is given this force in 5:16, we could read, "If anyone sees his brother *continually* sinning a sin . . . . " But how could someone see a brother *continually* sinning if one born of God does not *continually* sin?

It is apparent that the "tense solution" is an example of what in logic is called "special pleading." That is, it is selectively applied to 1 John 3:6 and 9 because they are problems, but not applied elsewhere even to the same kind of idea. Nor would those who propose this kind of approach welcome its use in other doctrinally significant places.

As an example, John 14:6 might be handled as some

wish to handle 1 John 3:6, 9. Then we could read this famous text as follows: "I am the way, the truth, and the life. No one *continually* comes to the Father except through Me." But the implication of this would be that *occasionally* someone might come another way! Obviously such an approach falsifies the text.

When the passage in which John's statements occur is closely considered, it is clear that the writer intends them to be taken in an absolute sense. Immediately before verse 6, he says:

> And you know that He was manifested to
> take away our sins, and in Him there is no sin
> (3:5).

Clearly, the declaration "in Him there is no sin" is an absolute denial of sin in the Son of God. But this is followed at once by the statement, "Whoever abides in Him does not sin." The point unmistakably is: if you abide in a sinless Person, you do not sin.[12]

The same can really be said also of 1 John 3:9. The reason one who is born of God does not sin is that "His seed remains in him; and he cannot sin, because he has been born of God." In other words, the regenerate one is sinless because he is begotten by a sinless Parent. It is completely contrary to the intent of the author to water such statements down. A sinless Parent does not beget a child who only sins a little! To say this, is in fact to deny what the text intends to communicate.

But how are such claims to be harmonized with the direct statement of 1:8 that no believer can claim to be sinless? There seems to be one simple way in which this can be done. The claims of 3:6 and 9 pertain to the believer when he is viewed only as "abiding" or as one who is "born of God." That is, sin is never the product of our abiding experience. It is never the act of the regenerate self per se.

On the contrary, sin is the product of ignorance and blindness toward God. "Whoever sins has neither seen Him nor known Him" (3:6b). When a believer sins, he is acting out of darkness, not out of knowledge.[13] He is acting as a man of flesh, not as a regenerate person.

Not surprisingly, even Paul could view sin as something fundamentally foreign to his true inner self. So, in recounting his personal struggle against sin in Romans 7, he can write:

> Now if I do what I will not to do, **it is no longer I who do it**, but sin that dwells in me. I find then a law, that evil is present with me, the one who wills to do good. For I delight in the law of God according to the inward man. But I see another law in my members, warring against the law of my mind, and bringing me into captivity to the law of sin which is in my members. O wretched man that I am! Who will deliver me from this body of death? I thank God – through Jesus Christ our Lord! So then, with the mind **I myself** serve the law of God, but **with the flesh** the law of sin (Rom. 7:20-25; emphasis added).

In this significant text, the Apostle discloses a self-perspective in which he can actually admit that he sins and yet still say that "it is no longer I who do it." His true self ("I myself," verse 25) serves God's law, even while he confesses that "with the flesh" he serves the law of sin.

It is of great importance that this form of self-analysis precedes the solution to his problem which is given in Romans 8. To view sin as basically foreign to what we are as regenerate people in Christ, is to take the first step toward spiritual victory over it.

From a slightly different perspective, the same conclusion can be drawn for the statement found in Galatians 2:20:

> I have been crucified with Christ; it is no longer I who live, but Christ lives in me.

But if only Christ truly lives, sin cannot be a part of that experience at all. If the person sins in whom Christ lives, that sin is in no way a part of that person's fundamental life, since Christ is that life.[14]

It is the final irony that the "tense solution" not only mishandles the linguistics of the text, but undermines its true force and power. By adopting an interpretation that tolerates a "moderate amount" of sin, this view destroys the author's point. *All sin* is the fruit of blindness and ignorance toward God (3:6b). It is satanic since "the devil has sinned from the beginning" (3:8). To make *any sin* less than these things, is to soften its character and to prepare the ground for tolerating it.

When everything is considered, the "tense solution" is a logical and theological quagmire. No wonder that the most recent major commentaries on 1 John abandon it. The "tense solution" is an idea whose time has come – and gone![15]

It follows from what has been said, that if a regenerate man *cannot* sin *at all* as a regenerate man (but only as an expression of his sinful flesh), he can never *manifest* his true inward nature by any other means than righteousness. By contrast, a "child of the devil" manifests his nature through sin.

This is precisely what John goes on to say in 3:10a:

> By this the children of God are manifest and
> the children of the devil (Greek).

The key word here is "manifest." A sinning Christian *conceals* his true character when he sins and *reveals* it only through holiness. On the other hand, a "child" of Satan *reveals* his true character by sin.

We should be cautious about calling all unsaved people "children of the devil." This kind of designation is rare in the NT and seems confined to those who are Satan's direct agents in a religious context (Mt. 13:35, 38, 39; Acts 13:10). For John, the expression "children of the devil" probably refers to the antichrists.[16]

Clearly, John wishes his readers to manifest their true nature by being victorious over sin. They are to shun the ideas and conduct of the Devil's children.

God's Children:
Loving and Hating

The words "by this" (3:10a; NKJV="in this") appear to round off the discussion found in 3:1-9. At 3:10b, a new thrust appears.[17] It builds, of course, on what has just been said.

If *all sin* – of whatever kind or extent – is satanic, it follows that it never finds its source in God. The one who does it, therefore, is not "of God" in the sinful thing that he does. This does not mean that such a person is unsaved. It means rather that he is acting outside of all vital contact with God. Satan, not God, is the source of his actions.[18]

Therefore, John goes on to say:

> Whoever does not do righteousness is not
> of God, nor is he who does not love his
> brother (3:10b, Greek).

That these words are intended for Christians is obvious on their face. The words "his brother" indicate this quite plainly. An unsaved man cannot hate *his* Christian brother since a true Christian is not really *his* brother. If John was thinking of unregenerate people, he could easily have said: "nor is he who does not love *a* brother." The fact that he personalizes the relationship with the word "his" must not be overlooked.

Quite naturally John appeals to the commandment given to Christians to "love one another" (3:11). He warns against brotherly hatred such as Cain exhibited toward Abel and describes such hatred as Satanic (3:12a). He touches a sensitive nerve when he suggests that this hatred can arise from the superior character of our brother's righteousness (3:12b). Such hatred is also worldly, and its presence in people of the world should occasion no surprise (3:13). Only its presence in believers is abnormal!

At this point the writer slips into the first person plural.

> **We** know that **we** have passed from death
> to life, because **we** love the brethren (3:14a;
> emphasis added).

This is followed by the warning that,

> He who does not love his brother abides in
> death (3:14b).

It is likely that the "we" of the first half of the verse is the familiar apostolic "we" of the epistle (cf. 1:1-5; 4:6).[19] The writer would thus be claiming that love of the brethren characterizes the apostolic circle to which he himself belongs. The Apostles find their experience in the sphere of "life." Anyone who hates a brother is living in the sphere of death to which also the world belongs.

(Here [in 3:14b] the Greek has no word for "his" before "brother." The statement is applicable to anyone – saved or unsaved – who hates a Christian brother.)

It is quite true that the expression "passed from death to life" occurs elsewhere in John 5:24. But that is the only other place in the NT where it does occur, outside of the present instance. So it is hardly a stereotyped or fixed expression even for John. The context here suggests that John is using it in an experiential sense and not with reference to conversion.

John means to say that he and his fellow Apostles know that they are operating in a sphere which can be described as "life" because they actually love their brothers in Christ. If anyone does not love a brother he is clearly "abiding" in the sphere of death. That is to say, he is out of touch with God. (This is true whether a man is saved or unsaved.) He is not living as a disciple of Jesus Christ (cf. John 13:35).

There follows a verse that has perplexed many. In it John asserts:

> Whoever hates his brother is a murderer,
> and you know that no murderer has eternal
> life abiding in him (3:15).

The idea that a Christian cannot commit murder encounters insuperable obstacles. For one thing, King David was guilty of murder in a fully literal sense. Moreover, upon confession of that sin, God forgave him (2 Samuel 12:13; see Psalm 51 and 1 John 1:9). Even Peter feels it necessary to warn his Christian readers against murder (1 Peter 4:15). In the face of such facts, it is plain that a genuine believer is not immune even to this sin.

If anyone were to maintain, nevertheless, that a Christian not only cannot commit murder, but he cannot even hate his brother, such a view would be totally lacking in Biblical realism. It is also quite contrary to actual Christian experience, as anybody who is fully honest must confess.

But John does not say that a murderer does not *have* eternal life. He says that a murderer does not have eternal life *abiding* in him. Since, for John, eternal life is nothing else than Christ Himself (cf. John 14:6; 1 John 1:2 and 5:20), this is the same as saying that "no murderer has *Christ* abiding in him."

Thus the key word in 1 John 3:14, 15 is once again the word "abide." In the sense in which this word is used in John 15 and everywhere in this epistle, this is a conditional experience dependent upon the Christian's obedience to God's commands. If a believer disobeys the command to "love one another" (3:11), he cannot claim to be "abiding" in the sphere of "life" or to have God's life "abiding" in him. Hatred breaks our *experiential contact* with the life of Christ, plunges us into spiritual darkness, and endows us with a quality of existence which can best be described as "death."[20]

As always, Paul also thought along these lines. When he attempted to live the Christian life under the law he discovered that "sin, taking occasion by the commandment, deceived me, and by it *killed me*" (Rom. 7:11; emphasis added). In fact, speaking to Christians directly he states:

> And if Christ is in you, the body is dead
> because of sin, but the Spirit is life because
> of righteousness (Rom. 8:10).

But if even the Christian's body may be called dead in a spiritual sense, what will the Christian experience if he lives according to the dictates of the body? The answer is obvious: he will have an experience that can be described as "death." Thus Paul goes on to warn: "For if you live according to the flesh *you will die*" (Rom. 8:13; emphasis added).

It is clear, therefore, that the Christian only *experiences* the eternal life God has freely given him when he is obedient to God. All else is an experience of *death* – at a spiritual level, first of all, but if continued in long enough, at a physical level as well (Jam. 1:15; Prov. 11:19; etc.).

In 1 John 3:10b-15, the Apostle's point is really quite simple. The failure to love one's brother is not a true experience of eternal life at all. It is an experience of moral murder and of death.[21] This is putting it quite starkly, but it furnishes an effective antidote to inward tendencies which every honest believer will admit that he has.

Let us return for a moment to the statement of 1 John 4:7. If a person truly loves his fellow Christians, he shows thereby that he is both "born of God and knows God." If he does not, then he surely does not really *know* God at the level of real fellowship and intimacy with Christ.

Of course, the unsaved world does not know God either. The believer who harbors hatred toward another believer is stepping into the same sphere of spiritual darkness and death where unsaved people live and operate. This by no means calls his salvation into question, but it firmly negates every claim to intimacy with the Father and the Son. In the final analysis, it is this intimacy that the epistle of 1 John is all about (1:3, 4).

Conclusion

In conclusion, therefore, it must be emphasized that the First Epistle of John is both internally consistent and fully harmonious with the uncomplicated offer of eternal life presented in the Fourth Gospel.

But the epistle will continue to be misunderstood by those who insist on equating "fellowship" and "abiding" with "regeneration" and "being a Christian." Once these unjustified equations are made, the message of John's letter is hopelessly obscured. The theological conclusions that arise as a result are fundamentally and irreconcilably hostile to the simple Biblical Gospel. In fact, they clash with the offer of assurance of salvation based on the testimony and promise of God alone.

It is in this way that the Apostle's powerful letter about fellowship has been sadly distorted and violently thrust into service in the siege of the Gospel.

CHAPTER

6

HEBREWS 6 AND 10:
THE CHRISTIAN AND APOSTASY

One of the most shocking questions in the Bible is recorded in Matthew 11:3: "Are You the Coming One, or do we look for another?"

The reason we find this question astounding is because it came from John the Baptist himself. The man who asked it was the same one who had once announced, "Behold! The Lamb of God who takes away the sin of the world!" (John 1:29). He had also declared, "And I have seen and testified that this is the Son of God" (John 1:34). But this faith was clearly not present in the question, "Are You the Coming One?"

Of course, John was in prison at the time (Matt. 11:2). No doubt his drained physical and mental condition contributed to the doubts he was experiencing. But one thing is plain. For the moment, his faith in Christ had failed.

Was he now a lost man? Of course not. To the woman at the well of Sychar, to the rabbi Nicodemus, to all His hearers, Jesus had offered a gift to be appropriated by faith. It was the gift that was permanent, not necessarily the faith that laid hold of it to begin with. "But the water that I shall give him [not the faith that claims it!] will become in him a fountain of water springing up into everlasting life" (John 4:14).

Faith is Fragile

Many present-day Christians think that the faith of a genuine believer cannot fail. But this is not an idea that can be supported from the New Testament. On the contrary, we learn the opposite from a statement found in 2 Timothy 2:17, 18:

> And their message will spread like cancer. Hymenaeus and Philetus are of this sort, who have strayed concerning the truth, saying that the resurrection is already past, and they **overthrow the faith** of some (emphasis added).

The Apostle Paul obviously knew of actual cases where the faith of individuals had been overthrown by false teaching. Yet, as the following verse makes clear, Paul is sure that such a calamity does not affect anyone's eternal destiny. He writes:

> Nevertheless the solid foundation of God stands, having this seal: "The Lord knows those who are His," and , "Let everyone who names the name of Christ depart from iniquity" (2:19).

It is obviously true, of course, that God knows *who* are His. But this observation is so self-evident that it is not likely to be Paul's meaning. Instead, the Greek word for "know" can imply relationship, and the Apostle's statement is best understood in this sense. God knows intimately and personally all who stand in relationship to Himself. This fact is undisturbed even when the believer's faith wavers or is overthrown.[1]

Moreover, the reality just stated in no way compromises God's holiness. His demand remains unaffected: "Let everyone who names the name of Christ depart from iniquity." But these words are a *command*, while the words preceding them are a statement of fact. It is not said that the command is always heeded. The following verses (2:20-21) show that in God's house it is *not* always heeded. Nevertheless the demand remains.

Paul's words show clearly that human faith is fragile but that God's relationship to those who exercise that faith is permanent. To confuse the stability of a man's faith[2] with the stability of God's purposes is to confuse two different things.   Naturally, such confusion leads inevitably to doctrinal error.

Apostasy in Hebrews 6

If this simple distinction had been kept in mind, the Epistle to the Hebrews could have been taken by the Church at face value. Its solemn warnings against apostasy could have had their intended effect. Instead, that epistle has suffered much at the hands of expositors who felt, no doubt sincerely, that true Christians could not really give in to the dangers the writer of Hebrews describes.

As is well known, in Hebrews 6:4, 5, the author describes individuals "who were once enlightened, and have tasted the heavenly gift, and have become partakers of the Holy Spirit, and have tasted the word of God and the powers of the age to come." These phrases very naturally describe real Christians. This will be obvious to all who have not already decided that the remainder of the passage cannot refer to Christians.

It seems almost needless to refute in detail the efforts made to show that unregenerate people are in view here. All such efforts are strained and unconvincing.

However, it is worth noting that to take the word "tasted" as an inadequate appropriation (in contrast to "eating"), is an idea clearly without foundation in this epistle. According to the author, "Jesus . . . was made a little lower than the angels . . . that He, by the grace of God, might taste death for everyone" (Heb. 2:9). No one will maintain that the Savior's "taste" of death was anything but the most profound experience of death. The idea of "tasting" is also a recognizable Biblical figure for genuine appropriation of God's goodness (see 1 Peter 2:1-3;

Psalm 34:8). To take the word in another sense in Hebrews 6:4, 5 has no valid support whatsoever.[3]

Additionally, the Greek verb for "enlightened" (6:4) is used again later in the letter to describe the readers' conversion experience ("illuminated," 10:32), while the term "partakers" (6:4) also describes their relationship to their heavenly calling (3:1). On all grounds the effort to see unsaved people in this text is extremely unnatural.[4]

But those whom the writer describes in 6:4, 5, can "fall away." This fact is partially concealed by the familiar English translation, "if they shall fall away" (6:6). Actually there is no word for "if" in the Greek text and none is required in the English translation. The verb form which is rendered "fall way" is a Greek participle which stands last in a series of participles. The first of these participles is represented by the words "those who were once enlightened" (verse 4). We ought to translate as follows:

> For it is impossible to renew to repentance
> those who were once enlightened, and
> have tasted the heavenly gift, and have
> become partakers of the Holy Spirit, and
> have tasted the good word of God and the
> powers of the age to come, and **have
> fallen away** . . . (emphasis added).

The writer clearly talks as if he knew of such cases.

However, we should not understand "falling away" here as though it meant the loss of eternal life. This conclusion (so frequently drawn) is unwarranted. The author repeatedly urges his readers to maintain their Christian profession and confidence (cf. 3:6, 12-15; 6:11, 12; 10:23-25). The man who "falls away" is evidently the one who casts away his Christian confidence with its promise of "great reward" (10:35).

Here again we meet the fragile nature of human faith. Man's faith needs continual nurture and admonition. Apart from that, apostasy is possible.[5]

The author states that the man who "falls away" is

impossible to "renew to repentance." This suggests a hardness of heart which resists all attempts to woo the man back to faith. But the writer probably thinks only of the normal efforts which other Christians may make to do this. This impossibility can hardly apply to God. In fact, in the metaphor which follows (vss. 7-8), the author plainly implies the possibility of restoration after punishment has been experienced.

The image which he uses is of a field which partakes of the rain of heaven and brings forth fitting fruits (6:7). In that case, the field enjoys divine blessing. On the other hand, "if it bears thorns and briers, it is rejected and near to being cursed, whose end is to be burned" (6:8).[6]

The burning of fields was a practice known in antiquity and would doubtless be a familiar idea to the readers of the epistle. But this practice was not designed to destroy the field, but to destroy the unacceptable growth which made it unfruitful. By using such an illustration the author clearly signals the ultimate purpose of God's judgment on the apostate Christian. That purpose is restoration to fruitfulness.[7]

This in no way makes the anticipation of judgment a pleasant one. On the contrary, it is a fearful expectation (see 10:26, 27). The guilt of the apostate is enormous since his renunciation of the faith is like a personal re-crucifixion of God's Son in which his Savior is openly shamed once again (6:6b). His life as an apostate meets with divine rejection and falls under a curse which is realized in the retribution to which he is now exposed (6:8). One might recall in this connection the "curses" which fell on God's Old Testament people as a result of their disobedience to the covenant of their God (see Deuteronomy 27:9-26).

Apostasy in Hebrews 10

Hebrews 10:26-39 must be understood in essentially the same way. This famous passage follows a call to "hold fast the confession of our hope without wavering" (10:23) and a warning against "forsaking the assembling of ourselves together, as is the manner of some" (10:25). The "willful" sinning of 10:26 is thus to be understood specifically of this kind of sin, namely, abandonment of the Christian faith and of the church. And this is said to be "after we have received the knowledge of the truth."

In other words, the writer again addresses the problem of apostasy.[8]

The author warns that to abandon Christianity is to abandon the only sacrifice (the death of Christ) which affords real protection and that apart from this "there no longer remains a sacrifice for sins" (10:26b). To take so fateful a step is to stand exposed to God's "fiery indignation." It is to range oneself with "the adversaries" of the Christian faith and to share in their calamities (10:27). But nothing in verses 26 and 27 ought to be taken as a reference to hell.

The punishment which the author predicts for the apostate will be a "worse punishment" than the summary execution which offenders against the Mosaic law experienced (10:28, 29a). Of course, there are many forms of retribution which are "worse" than swift death. The writer of Lamentations gives eloquent expression to this reality (Lam. 4:6, 9). One thinks readily of the mental disorder that afflicted Saul in the period of his declining years. Lingering illness, loss of loved ones, and many other experiences might be mentioned. The writer, however, is not concerned with being specific. He is only concerned with warning about the severity of the retribution which an apostate has in store for him.

But it is precisely because the apostate is a Christian that his crime is so great. This point is forcefully driven home by the words of verse 29:

> Of how much worse punishment, do you suppose, will he be thought worthy who has trampled the Son of God underfoot, counted the blood of the covenant **by which he was sanctified** a common

thing, and insulted the Spirit of grace
(emphasis added).

In the words "by which he was sanctified" the writer
makes it inescapable that he is speaking of Christians.

The author has already spoken about sanctification in
the immediately preceding context of Hebrews 10. His
statements show clearly what he means by this idea:

> By that will we have been sanctified through
> the offering of the body of Jesus Christ once
> for all (10:10).

> For by one offering He has perfected forever
> those who are sanctified (10:14).

It follows that in describing the apostate as one who has
"counted the blood of the covenant by which he was
sanctified a common thing," the writer is describing one
who has been "perfected forever."[9] Precisely for this
reason, his apostasy is an enormous offense against
divine grace.   It fully merits the "worse punishment"
which the author predicts.

All attempts to deny that a real Christian is in view
here can only be described as a refusal to face the author's
true meaning.   The explanation that the "he" in the
expression "by which he was sanctified" refers to Christ
has absolutely nothing to commend it.   No impartial
reader could so understand the text.   Futhermore, in
Hebrews, Christ is not described as sanctified, but as the
Sanctifier (2:11).[10] The writer of Hebrews obviously
believes that a true Christian can apostatize.[11]

The remainder of the passage (10:30-36) reinforces this
point. Vengeance and judgment await the apostate (vss.
30-31). But the readers can be strengthened against such
failure by the recollection of their former fidelity in time
of trial (vss. 32-34).   This past confidence is to be
maintained now: "Therefore do not cast away your
confidence, which has great reward" (vs. 35). What they
need is "endurance" so that they may accomplish God's

will and receive the reward He has promised (verse 36).
The coming of Christ draws near (verse 37) and this should
give them courage to hold on.

Of particular interest is the statement of verse 38:

> Now the just shall live by faith; but if **h e**
> draws back, my soul has no pleasure in him
> (Greek).

The words are drawn from Habbakuk 2:3, 4 and include
the famous Pauline proof-text about justification by faith.

But the writer does not introduce this quotation with a
formula of citation like "the Scripture says," etc. There is
a good reason why he does not. What he has done is to
alter the form of the Old Testament reference in a way that
fits the context of his thought. In that sense the statement
of verse 38 is more strictly an Old Testament "allusion"
than an Old Testament "quotation."

In this altered form it is plain that it is the "just" one
who may draw back.[12] If so, of course, God will not be
pleased with him. The words "my soul has no pleasure in
him" are a figure of speech called *litotes*. In litotes a
positive idea is expressed by negating its opposite. As the
larger context makes plain, the meaning is, "God will be
severely angered" (see verse 27).[13]

Verse 39 is misleading in its present English form.
The Greek word for "perdition" is not (as is sometimes
claimed) a technical term for "hell." Instead it may be used
of simple waste (Matt. 26:8; Mk. 14:4) or of execution (Acts
25:16). In secular Greek its fundamental meanings were
"destruction," "ruin," and similar ideas. Likewise, the
particular Greek expression rendered "the saving of the
soul" does not occur elsewhere in Biblical Greek. It is not
the same Greek phrase which we met in James 1:21. But
the precise phrase used here is found in classical Greek
with the meaning "to save the life."[14] The verse might be
more appropriately translated:

> But we for our part [the Greek pronoun is

emphatic] are not of those who draw back to
ruin, but of those who have faith for the
saving of our life.

In this sense the verse fits perfectly with the larger
context. The apostate faces disaster and ruin. His
punishment may not be swift execution as under Moses'
law (cf. 10:28), but the judgment he experiences could
easily end in death as other sin also does (Jam. 1:15; 5:20;
Prov. 10:27, 11:19; etc.). But faith is the means by which
the "just one" lives and is therefore indispensable to the
preservation of his life (cf. 10:38).

From verse 32 through 36 the author has used the
second person plural "you" to address his readers. The
swift change to an emphatic "we" in verse 39 appears to be
a reference to himself. The cultured, literary "we" is the
author's regular way of indicating himself (see 2:5; 5:11;
6:9, 11; 8:1; 13:18). The writer seems to be stating his own
intention to hold on to his Christian profession and hope.
He means something like: "But we ourselves (= I myself) do
not belong among the number who draw back, but among
those who preserve their lives by a continuing faith."[15]

It is a fitting conclusion to a passage on the "willful"
sin of apostasy. The sin of apostasy (i.e., turning away
from Christianity) can only be taken deliberately. The
refusal to take it is equally deliberate. The author has
definitely decided not to take it. He trusts that his readers
will refuse to do so as well.

Apostasy in Hebrews 3

The Epistle to the Hebrews, therefore, is
fundamentally concerned with the problem of those who
draw back from their Christian commitment and
conviction. Those who do so, of course, abandon the
church (cf. 10:25). It is therefore the *visible household of
faith* from which they withdraw. They cannot withdraw
from the family of God, however. Precisely for this reason
they are subject to God's discipline.

If the epistle is read in this way, it offers no fundamental problems at all. It clashes in no way with the basic truths of the Gospel. Christians in the local church are in active partnership with the Apostle and High Priest of their Christian profession. They must take care to hold on to this partnership.

In 3:1, the word "partakers" is used to describe this relationship. The Greek word can refer to business partners and this is its actual meaning in its only New Testament occurrence outside of Hebrews (Luke 5:7). It is common in the Greek papyri in this sense.[16] But "partnership" with Christ is a priestly occupation in which there is a spiritual altar that offers spiritual food (13:10) and in which there are spiritual sacrifices to be made (13:15, 16). One must hold on to this role.

If the Christian withdraws from the visible, functioning priestly household, that is, from the church itself, he ceases to be a "partner of Christ." This is the meaning of the statement in 3:14 where the word for "partaker" is the same word as the one used in verse 1:

> For we have become partakers [partners] of Christ if we hold the beginning of our confidence steadfast to the end (3:14).[17]

The same truth is also stated in verse 6:

> . . . whose house we are if we hold fast the confidence and the rejoicing of the hope firm to the end (3:6).

Thus we participate in the visible household of faith, in partnership with Christ, only so long as we hold fast to our Christian confidence and hope. If we cast away this confidence and withdraw from the house, we cast away the privileges that belong to the "house." This is like a son in an earthly household who leaves home and ceases to be an active partner in that home, even though he does not thereby cease to be a son.[18]

No doubt the warnings of Hebrews against abandonment of the faith are sharp and forceful. But this is no reason to deny that they apply to us. Indeed, this kind of denial robs them of the impact they were intended to have. When the exhortations of the epistle are redirected toward supposed "false professors of faith," they are in reality distorted.

The author of Hebrews shows not the slightest trace of a belief that his audience might contain unsaved people. Instead, he persistently addresses them as brethren (3:1, 12; 10:19; 13:22) who share the heavenly calling (3:1) and who have an High Priest through whom they can approach the throne of grace (4:14-16). The suggestion that he nevertheless thinks some of his audience are unregenerate is not founded on anything at all in the text.

Conclusion

No doubt the conclusions reached in this chapter will be stoutly resisted by those who cannot believe that a Christian could abandon his faith. But we insist that refusing to admit this possibility is an obvious begging of the question. The view that a Christian cannot apostatize is at bottom an arbitrary theological conviction. Since it is note supported by the Bible, it ought to be given up.

When this is done, many passages can be read in their normal sense and the warnings they contain can be directly faced. Moreover, we can then also hear a note of hope for those whose faith has suffered shipwreck. It is such a note that sounds in the solemn statements Paul makes in 1 Timothy 1:19, 20:

> . . . having faith and a good conscience, which some having rejected, concerning the faith have suffered shipwreck, of whom are Hymenaeus and Alexander, whom I have delivered to Satan that they may learn not to blaspheme.

What is striking here is that the Greek word translated

"learn" literally means "to be trained," "to be educated." It is a normal Greek word for the education of a child who is a minor. Its only other uses by Paul are all in reference to Christians (1 Cor. 11:32; 2 Cor. 6:9; 2 Tim 2:25; Titus 2:12). 2 Timothy 2:25 is no exception to this.

Clearly the most natural understanding here is that Paul regarded Hymenaeus and Alexander as Christians whose false doctrine amounted to blasphemy. They are now under divine discipline for which Satan is the instrument. (One might compare with this Paul's similar concept in 1 Corinthians 5:4, 5.) Paul hopes that the outcome of this spiritual education will be that these men will renounce their false doctrine.[19]

It is quite natural to suspect that this Hymenaeus is the same as the one mentioned in 2 Timothy 2:17 and who taught that the resurrection was already past. Whether in the end the discipline had a positive effect on either himself or Alexander, is a matter on which the Scripture is silent. But the element of hope remains, just as it did also in the metaphor of the burnt field in Hebrews 6:7, 8.

Nevertheless, the tragic dangers of doctrinal shipwreck remain a grim reality in the history of the Church and in its contemporary experience. A disservice is done to the cause of Christ when it is claimed that such dangers do not exist for real Christians.

"Therefore let him who thinks he stands take heed lest he fall" (1 Cor. 10:12).

CHAPTER

7

PROBLEM PASSAGES IN PAUL

Certain passages in the Pauline letters have been taken to prove that perseverance in good works is an inevitable outcome of genuine saving faith. As has already been pointed out, this kind of idea destroys the believer's ground of assurance. A man who must wait for works to verify his faith cannot know until life's end whether or not his faith was real. This leads to the absurd conclusion that a man can believe in Christ without knowing whether he has believed in Christ!

Naturally the Pauline texts in question are all consistent with his fundamental doctrine of justification by faith apart from works. When the Apostle writes that it is "not by works of righteousness which we have done, but according to His mercy He saved us" (Tit. 3:5), his true conviction comes through clearly. Paul could never have so expressed himself if he had regarded works as the real means by which we can know we are saved. To the contrary, he directs our focus away from the works *we* have done to the mercy of *God*. How can anyone read Paul and still believe that we can only be sure of God's mercy by our works?

Similarly, Paul also writes, "But to him who *does not work* but believes on Him who justifies the ungodly, his faith is accounted for righteousness" (Rom. 4:5; emphasis added). Can anyone imagine that Paul would then go on to add, "But you need to work or you will not know whether you have been justified or not"! Such a proposition is a monstrous distortion of Pauline truth. Any articulation of the Gospel which can affirm such a thing ought to be forcefully rejected by the Christian Church.

In the next few pages some Pauline statements will be examined which are claimed to lead to the result we have just criticized. A few others will be considered in Chapter 9 in connection with the subject of heirship. The first text that claims attention here is Galatians 6:8.

Galatians 6:8

In Galatians 6:7-9 Paul writes as follows:

> Do not be deceived, God is not mocked; for whatever a man sows, that he will also reap. For he who sows to his flesh will of the flesh reap corruption, but he who sows to the Spirit will of the Spirit reap everlasting life. And let us not grow weary while doing good, for in due season we shall reap if we do not lose heart.

It is important to see exactly what this text says. "Everlasting life," Paul states, is the direct consequence of sowing to the Spirit, of doing good. Corruption is what you reap if you do evil. It is all part of the law of the harvest. A man gets what he deserves to get.

It goes almost without saying that there is nothing said here about the "inevitable" results of saving faith. Indeed, the hortatory thrust of the passage shows the opposite. The Galatians must be careful about how they sow. They must never suppose that they can "mock" God or avoid the inexorable law of the harvest. The final reaping is not a foregone conclusion, but rather it is contingent on not "growing weary" while doing good.

But equally there is nothing here about justification by faith or the concept of a free gift. Nothing is plainer than that the "everlasting life" of which Paul speaks is not free, but based on the moral merits of those who reap it. To deny this is to deny the most obvious aspect of the text.

All becomes clear, however, if we simply remember that the Apostle is addressing believers (see, for example, 3:2-5) who have already been justified by faith and who possess everlasting life as a free gift. Naturally Paul knew that eternal life was freely given (Rom. 6:23; see also Rom. 5:15-18), just as the Apostle John knew this. But Paul is not speaking about what the Galatians *already have*, but about what they may *yet receive*. Herein lies the key to this text.

(1) The Nature of Eternal Life

It must not be forgotten that eternal life is nothing less than the very life of God Himself. As such it cannot be thought of as a mere fixed and static entity. Rather, its potentialities are rich beyond the power of the mind to conceive them. Thus we find Jesus declaring, "I have come that they may have life, and that they may have it *more abundantly*" (John 10:10). From this we learn that eternal life can be experienced in more than one measure or degree.

But it cannot be experienced at all unless first received as a free gift. Not surprisingly, the Creator of the universe has illustrated this with every human life that is born into the world.

No man or woman possesses physical life at all except by his parents imparting it to him. Even physical life, therefore, is a free gift! But when a child is born into this present world, the capacities of human life (all present at birth) must be developed by himself under the guidance of his parents and subsequent teachers. How "abundantly" he will experience human life is determined by his response to instruction and to experience itself.

So it is in the spiritual realm too. In order to have life "more abundantly," one must meet the conditions for this. One must respond properly to his heavenly Parent.

Here it should be stated clearly that in the New Testament eternal life is presented both as a free gift and as a reward merited by those who earn it.   But one important distinction always holds true.   Wherever eternal life is viewed as a reward, it is obtained in the future. But wherever eternal life is presented as a gift, it is obtained in the present.

Naturally, it goes without saying that no one can ever receive eternal life as a reward who does not first accept it as a free gift. This is the same as saying that a person must first *have* life before he can experience it richly.

(2) Harvesting Eternal Life

If Galatians 6:8 is understood as speaking only of a man's final salvation from hell, then it teaches clearly that this final salvation is by works. Not to admit this is not to be candid. But no one excludes works from his doctrine of salvation more vigorously than Paul does, and he insists that to mix works and grace is to alter the character of both (see Rom. 11:6).

Galatians 6:8 is irreconcilable with fundamental Pauline truth so long as one holds the view that final salvation is under discussion.

But why hold this view? It is easy to understand how the measure and extent of one's experience of God's life must depend on the measure of his response to God. From that perspective the image of a harvest is exactly right. The nature and quantity of the seed we sow determines the nature and quantity of the harvest.

It is obviously wise for a Christian to be reminded that every act he performs is like a seed sown in a field. Its harvest will be either corruption or eternal life.[2] And is there a Christian alive who has not sown much more often to his flesh than he ought to have done? Clearly the Church needs this reminder about the law of life. To make the issue here a man's final destiny in heaven or hell is to lose the whole point of the exhortation.

If the matters just discussed are kept in mind, other passages which offer eternal life as a future experience based on works can be understood in their proper bearing. One might think especially of Matthew 19:29 with its parallels in Mark 10:30 and Luke 18:30. The eschatological "harvest" is in view in these places. Obedient men reap an experience of eternal life precisely because they are obedient.[3] But this in no way conflicts with the reality that such obedience must be preceded by, and motivated through, a gift of life given freely and without any condition but faith alone.

Colossians 1:21-23

Colossians 1:23 has sometimes been taken to teach that perseverance in the faith is a condition for final salvation. The passage reads as follow:

> And you, who once were alienated and enemies in your mind by wicked works, yet now He has reconciled in the body of His flesh through death, to present you holy, and blameless, and above reproach in His sight – if indeed you continue in the faith, grounded and steadfast, and are not moved away from the hope of the gospel which you have heard . . . (1:21-23a).

It is clear that "condition" is the only appropriate word here. There is nothing to support the view that perseverance in the faith is an "inevitable" outcome of true salvation. On the contrary, the text reads like a warning. Naturally, in the context of the Colossian heresy (Col. 2:8, 16-23) that is exactly what it is.[4]

But once again the mistake is made of referring the statement of the text to a man's final salvation. Words like "holy," "blameless," and "above reproach" do not require the sense of "sinless" or "absolutely perfect." Men can be described in all these ways who are not completely sinless. The word translated as "above reproach" is actually found in the Pauline list of qualifications for deacons and elders in the sense of "blameless" (1 Tim. 3:10; Titus 1:6, 7).

A comparison of Colossians 1:22 with 1:28 is also helpful. In 1:28 Paul writes:

> Him we preach, warning every man and teaching every man in all wisdom, that we may present every man perfect in Christ Jesus.

This statement is connected with 1:22 by the presence of the special word "present." But here Paul employs the word "perfect" which is the normal Greek word for "mature" (and is so used in 1 Cor. 2:6; 14:20; Heb. 5:14). Obviously this word also does not have to suggest sinless perfection.

It is natural, therefore, to see 1:22 and 1:28 as slightly different forms of the same idea. The aim of Christ's reconciling work at the cross is the aim Paul serves by his teaching ministry. He seeks to bring men to that matured experience of holiness which will enable them to be presented acceptably to God. When they stand on review before Him their lives ought to meet with His approval (see also Rom. 14:10-12; 2 Cor. 5:10).

But this approval can only be achieved, he cautions his readers, if they hold firmly to their faith in the Gospel and do not allow new ideas and doctrines to move them away from fundamental truths (1:23).[5]

As we have seen already, Paul knew perfectly well that Christians were not immune to the influences of heresy (2 Tim. 2:17-19; 1 Tim. 1:18-20). He is saying, then, that the Colossians will never reach maturity in holiness if they listen to the wrong voices. In that event, they could not be presented to God in a spiritual state which truly fulfilled the aims of the cross. Their lives would be open to His censure. They are, therefore, to hold firmly to the faith they had heard from the beginning.

But about perseverance in the faith as a condition for final salvation from hell, Paul here says nothing at all.

1 Corinthians 15:2

It might be thought, however, that such an idea *does* find expression in 1 Corinthians 15:1, 2. There Paul writes:

> Moreover, brethren, I declare to you the gospel which I preached to you, which also you received and in which you stand, by which also you are saved, if you hold fast that word which I preached to you – unless you believed in vain.

The problem in correctly understanding this verse is caused by the English translation. A very flexible Greek verb (*katecho*) is translated "hold fast" in the New King James Version (the AV has "keep in memory"). But the verb could equally well be rendered "take hold of" or "take possession of." In that case it would refer to the act of appropriating the truth of the Gospel by faith.[6]

Closer examination of the Greek text suggests that this is indeed the correct understanding. The Greek word order can be represented as follows: "by which also you are saved, by that word I preached to you, if you take hold of it, unless you believed in vain."[7] From this it appears that Paul is thinking of the saving effect of the preached word when it is duly appropriated, unless in fact that appropriation (by faith) has been in vain.

What he means by believing "in vain" is made clear in verses 14 and 17:

> And if Christ is not risen, then our preaching is empty and your faith is also empty [the AV has "vain" for "empty"].

> And if Christ is not risen, your faith is futile; you are still in your sins [the AV has "vain" for "futile"].[8]

First Corinthians 15:2 must be read in the light of the subsequent discussion about resurrection. Paul is simply saying, in verse 2, that the Gospel he has preached to them is a saving Gospel when it is appropriated by faith, unless, after all, the resurrection is false.   In that case, no salvation has occurred at all and the faith his readers had exercised was futile. But naturally Paul absolutely insists on the reality of the resurrection of Christ. He therefore does not think that the Corinthians have believed "in vain."

But neither here nor anywhere else in the Pauline letters can the Apostle be correctly understood as teaching that perseverance in the faith is a condition of, or an indispensable sign of, final salvation from hell.

1 Corinthians 1:8

In the opening chapter of his first letter to the Corinthian church, Paul speaks positively and hopefully about the church's spiritual prospects. The context shows clearly that he is speaking of the church corporately:

> I thank my God always concerning you for the grace of God which was given to you by Christ Jesus, that you were enriched in everything by Him in all utterance and all knowledge, even as the testimony of Christ was confirmed in you, so that you come short in no gift, eagerly waiting for the revelation of our Lord Jesus Christ, who will also confirm you to the end, that you may be blameless in the day of our Lord Jesus Christ. God is faithful, by whom you were called into the fellowship of His Son, Jesus Christ our Lord (1 Cor. 1:4-9).

Here the Corinthian church is praised because it is so richly endowed with spiritual gifts, because the testimony of Christ has received confirmation in the church's life and experience, and because it waits eagerly for the coming of Christ. Paul fully expects God to bring the church to the place where it is blameless before Him (the letter shows the church has a long way to go!), and he bases this expectation on God's faithfulness. Paul is sure that the many problems at Corinth, which he is about to discuss, can be worked out.

It would be a mistake to read more into the text than that. There is not to be found here a guarantee that each and every Christian individual will necessarily be brought to the place where his Christian life is "blameless" before God. (The word "blameless" is the same one we have met as "above reproach" in Colossians 1:22.) In Paul's mind no such guarantee existed.[9]

(1) Paul's View in 1 Corinthians 3

This is made perfectly plain in this very letter. In chapter 3 the Apostle describes the evaluation of the Christian's life and work which will someday take place at the Judgment Seat of Christ (see again, Rom. 14:10-12; 2 Cor. 5:10). His words are these:

> For no other foundation can anyone lay than that which is laid, which is Jesus Christ. Now if anyone builds on this foundation with gold, silver, precious stones, wood, hay, straw, each one's work will become clear; for the Day will declare it, because it will be revealed by fire; and the fire will test each one's work, of what sort it is. If anyone's work which he has built on it endures, he will receive a reward. If anyone's work is burned, he will suffer loss; but he himself will be saved, yet so as through fire (1 Cor. 3:11-15).

It is clear from this text that Paul entertained the possibility that in the Day of divine evaluation, a

Christian's work might be "burned up." The Greek verb employed in verse 15 (the one rendered "burned") is in fact an intensive word like our own verb "burned down." Should a Christian's works suffer such a fate, Paul insists that his eternal destiny nevertheless will not be affected. "But he himself will be saved, yet so as through fire."[10]

This declaration is so straightforward that it is absolutely amazing how widely it has been ignored. Obviously, if a believer's works are "burned down" he will not stand "blameless" before God. So 1:8 does not claim that a "blameless" state will be true of every Christian at the Judgment Seat of Christ. Paul was speaking primarily about the spiritual status which he expected the Corinthian church to achieve corporately.

(2) A Further Caution

But even here caution must be exercised not to make the words of 1:8 say more than they actually do.

If a counselor says to a troubled counselee, "God will strengthen you and see you through," this claim ought not to be taken as a flat and unconditional prediction. Instead it is an expression of the counselor's conviction that God can be relied upon by the troubled individual who needs Him. Naturally he expects the counselee to appropriate God's help in the proper ways.

In 1 Corinthians 1:4-9 Paul begins his epistle on a positive note. He commends in the Corinthian church what there is to commend (there was a great deal to criticize!), and he expresses the expectation that "God will confirm you [that is, 'give you strength'] to the end, that you may be blameless in the day of our Lord Jesus Christ." But it is implied in such a declaration that the Corinthians must *want* that strength and must appropriate it properly.

Paul's main point is that God will furnish the needed help, because He is faithful (verse 9). Those who have elevated the statement of 1:8 to the level of a theological claim about Christian perseverance have misunderstood Paul's meaning.[11] They have also created false theology.

Philippians 1:6

It has often been said that the Epistle to the Philippians is a "thank you note." The Philippians have sent a monetary gift to Paul for which he is deeply grateful (4:10-19). Naturally at the very beginning of the epistle he refers to their material generosity. In 1:3-6 he writes:

> I thank my God upon every remembrance of you, always in every prayer of mine making request for you all with joy, for your fellowship in the gospel from the first day until now, being confident of this very thing, that He who has begun a good work in you will complete it until the day of Jesus Christ.

It is natural to understand this passage in special reference to the Philippians' recent generosity. This is implied rather plainly by the Greek word "fellowship." This word very often refers to material "sharing" and can sometimes even mean "contribution" (see Rom. 15:26). Paul is assuring the Philippians that their "good work" of sharing in the spread of the Gospel will be carried to full fruitfulness by God. Its total effects (for example, in the winning of souls) will only be manifest in the day of Jesus Christ.

In fact, this very epistle can be seen as part of the fruit which that "good work" produced, since the Philippians' gift occasioned the letter. Whatever spiritual impact Paul's letter has had on the Church down through the centuries (who can calculate it?) is therefore part of the "interest" which has accumulated on this simple material investment in the cause of Christ.[12]

It may also be suggested that every good work which we do has a potential for usefulness that lies far beyond its original intent. God alone can "perfect" our good works and give them their full impact – often far beyond the lifetime of the one "in" whom the good work begins. Only the day of Jesus Christ will disclose all that God does with what we do for Him.

Philippians 1:6 is a lovely and thought-provoking utterance by an appreciative Apostle. But about the issue of Christian perseverance it has nothing to say at all.

Philippians 2:12, 13

Philippians 2:12, 13 are more relevant to the issues under discussion. In these verses Paul writes:

> Therefore, my beloved, as you have always obeyed, not as in my presence only, but now much more in my absence, work out your own salvation with fear and trembling; for it is God who works in you both to will and to do for His good pleasure.

It is clear that if the "salvation" Paul speaks of here refers to escape from hell, then obedient works are a *condition* for that. Once again it would be unwarranted to read into the passage the idea that such obedience is merely the evidence of true faith. That idea has nothing whatsoever to support it in the text. It can only amount to an evasion of the plain declaration that this "salvation" must be "worked out."

Whatever is involved here, it is manifestly salvation by works!

It follows that Paul must be talking about something quite different from the salvation he speaks of in Ephesians 2:8, 9 and Titus 3:4-7. As a matter of fact he is.

(1) Salvation Equals "Deliverance"

In only two other places in the epistle does Paul use the

term "salvation."   One of these is in 1:19, 20 where he writes:

> For I know that this will turn out for my
> deliverance [AV, "salvation"] through your
> prayer and the supply of the Spirit of Jesus
> Christ, according to my earnest expectation
> and hope that in nothing I shall be ashamed,
> but with all boldness, as always, so now also
> Christ will be magnified in my body, whether
> by life or by death.

The first century reader was not likely to have any problem understanding this.   The Greek word for "salvation" (*soteria*) simply meant "deliverance," as the NKJV now translates it here.   Like the English word "deliverance" it could have wide application and was particularly applicable to life-threatening situations. Paul now confronts a life-threatening situation in which the outcome of his impending trial cannot be predicted with absolute certainty.

His readers knew this, of course. When Paul writes, "I know that this will turn out for my deliverance," their first impression would be that he anticipated release from his imprisonment. But the remainder of his words show them that this is not what he has in mind. "For me," says Paul, "real 'deliverance' (or, "salvation") will consist of magnifying Christ whether I live or die. For this, I need your prayers and the help of God's Spirit."

In a very courageous way, therefore, Paul elevates his natural human concern with "deliverance" (or "salvation") from trouble to the level of a spiritual concern that he will be "delivered" (or "saved") from failing to honor God in whatever befalls him. In saying this, of course, he hopes to motivate his readers to a similar objective.

(2) The Parallel
in 1:27-30

In fact, that is exactly what he tries to do directly a little later in this chapter. In 1:27-30 he writes:

> Only let your conduct be worthy of the gospel of Christ, so that whether I come and see you or am absent, I may hear of your affairs, that you stand fast in one spirit, with one mind striving together for the faith of the gospel, and not in any way terrified by your adversaries, which is to them a proof of perdition [or, "ruin," as it could be translated] but to you of salvation [or, "deliverance"], and that from God. For to you it has been granted on behalf of Christ, not only to believe in Him, but also to suffer for His sake, having the same conflict which you saw in me and now hear is in me.

In this exhortation, the Apostle applies to the readers the idea he had earlier expressed concerning himself.

The Philippians also have sufferings just as he does. But they too can aspire to a "deliverance" (or "salvation") in which Christ is magnified in them as well. If they will stand unitedly for the Gospel and are not terrified by their adversaries, that will be proof that this "deliverance" (or "salvation") is being realized in their lives.

By contrast, their courage and fidelity foretell the ruin of their enemies, whether temporally or eternally.

Paul and his readers are aware that there is a "deliverance" (or "salvation") from hell which they have already obtained by faith in Christ. But the "deliverance" (or "salvation") he offers them here is over and above that which they already have. It is one that issues from sufferings.

Therefore, Paul can say, "For to you it has been granted . . . not only to believe in Him, but also to suffer for His sake." In other words, just as there is a salvation through faith, so there is one through suffering. That too is being granted to the Philippians.

But *this* "salvation" (or "deliverance") must be *worked*

out. It is the product of obedience even under the most trying of circumstances. When Philippians 2:12,13 is properly referred back to the Apostle's earlier references to "salvation," then its bearing becomes clear. Since this "salvation" consists essentially in honoring Christ by life or by death, it is necessarily inseparable from a life of obedience.

In the words that follow immediately in 2:14-16, the nature of this life is once more described. The Philippians are encouraged to be "children of God without fault in the midst of a crooked and perverse generation, among whom you shine as lights in the world" (2:15). Clearly, such a result would be a magnificent triumph, a kind of spiritual "deliverance" or "salvation," in the midst of a hostile and dangerous earthly situation.[13]

Interlude: Biblical Salvation

What we have just seen in Philippians is important for the Bible as a whole. The exact meaning of the term "salvation" must never be taken for granted.

(1) The Word for Salvation in the Greek Bible

When the Greek translation of the Old Testament is considered along with the Greek New Testament, it can safely be said that the most common meaning of the word "salvation" (*soteria*) in the Greek Bible is the one which refers to God's deliverance of His people from their trials and hardships. This meaning is widespread in Psalms especially. Among the references which can be cited are Psalm 3:8; 18:3, 35, 46, 50; 35:3; 37:39; 38:22; 44:4; etc. In all these places, and many more besides, the Greek Old Testament uses the word *soteria* ("salvation").

First century Christians, therefore, were every bit as likely to understand a reference to "salvation" in this sense as they were to understand it in the sense of "escaping from hell."

New Testament interpreters forget this fact *very* frequently. In place of careful consideration about the sense which the term "salvation" has in any given context, there is a kind of interpretive "reflex action" that automatically equates the word with final salvation from hell. This uncritical treatment of many New Testament passages has led to almost boundless confusion at both the expository and doctrinal levels.

Serious interpreters of the New Testament Scriptures must carefully avoid this kind of automatic response. They should seek to determine from the context the kind of "deliverance" in question. It may well be deliverance from death to life or from hell to heaven. But equally it may well be a deliverance from trial, danger, suffering or temptation. The context – sometimes the larger context of the book itself (as in Romans and Hebrews) – must determine the exact meaning.

(2) "Saving the Life" in the Bible

Furthermore, in the teaching of Jesus a distinctive note is sounded which is not really found in the Old Testament passages about "salvation." Although the Old Covenant saint thought instinctively of the preservation of his physical life, the New Covenant person is taught to go beyond this consideration.

According to Jesus, a man can "save his life" even when he "loses" it (see Matt. 16:25 and parallels). This paradox suggests that even death itself cannot destroy the value and worth of a life lived in discipleship to Christ. Such a life survives every calamity and results in eternal reward and glory.[14]

Paul is not far from such a thought in Philippians. To be truly "delivered" in suffering is not necessarily to survive it physically, but to glorify Christ through it.

The same idea is present in the Apostle Peter's famous

passage on suffering found in 1 Peter 1:6-9.   The expression in verse 9 which is translated "the salvation of your souls" would be much better translated according to its normal Greek sense: "the salvation of your lives." Peter is describing the messianic experience in which the believer partakes of Christ's sufferings first, in order that he might subsequently share the glory to which those sufferings lead (1 Peter 1:10, 11). In this way the "life" is saved, even when paradoxically it is lost, because it results in "praise honor, and glory at the revelation of Jesus Christ" (1 Pet. 1:7).[15]

In fact, it can be said that there is not a single place in the New Testament where the expression "to save the soul" ever means final salvation from hell.   It cannot be shown that any native Greek speaker would have understood this expression in any other than the idiomatic way.   That is, he would understand it as signifying "to save the life."

In modern use, of course, "to save the soul" is almost universally understood as a reference to eternal salvation. But this fixity in its meaning is not relevant to its New Testament use.   In the New Testament we should always understand it as equal to our expression: "to save the life."

In Philippians Paul never uses the word "salvation" to refer to the question of heaven or hell.   After all, both he and his readers *knew* where they were going.   Their names were in the Book of Life (Phil. 4:3)!

Romans 2:7, 10, 13

It is a tragic feature of the modern debate over salvation, that certain statements made by Paul in his great epistle to the church at Rome have been turned upside down.   These statements are found in Romans 2 and are intended by the Apostle to underline man's hopeless state before the bar of God's judgment.   Instead, some modern theologians take them as proof-texts that good works, as the fruit of faith, will be the final test of a person's salvation.[16]

Let us look at the Pauline statements in question:

> . . . who 'will render to every man according
> to his deeds': eternal life to those who by
> patient continuance in doing good seek for
> glory, honor, and immortality . . .
>
> . . . but glory, honor, and peace to everyone
> who works what is good, to the Jew first and
> also to the Greek.
>
> . . . for not the hearers of the law are just in
> the sight of God, but the doers of the law will
> be justified . . . (Rom. 2:6, 7, 10, 13).

It is certainly astounding that these words could be taken
in such a way as to nullify the doctrine Paul goes on to
teach in this epistle, when he writes emphatically:

> Therefore by the deeds of the law no flesh
> will be justified in His sight, for by the law is
> the knowledge of sin (Rom. 3:20).

This tragic confusion could have been easily avoided.
In Romans 2 Paul is discussing how God will deal with
men in the final judgment (Rom. 2:5).   One should
remember that born-again believers do not come into that
judgment (John 5:24).[17] At the judgment bar of God, the
day of grace will be past and men will stand before their
Judge for His final assessment of their lives (see Rev.
20:12). His judgment will be impartial and based on their
works.   Those who have persevered in doing good may
expect eternal life.   Those who have not only heard, but
kept, God's law, will receive God's justification.
  But who are these? There are none. Romans 3:20 says
so plainly. So does Romans 3:9-19 – very emphatically![18]
  The standpoint in Romans 2 is analogous to a judge
who has a line of defendants ranged before his tribunal.
Speaking in the non-prejudicial language of the law-
courts he might say to them: "In this courtroom everyone
will get exactly what he deserves. The innocent will be
cleared, but the guilty will be condemned to punishment."

Does this statement imply that some of the defendants *are* innocent and *will* be cleared? Of course not. The judge is simply stating the principles which will obtain in his court. Justice and equity will be the hallmarks of this judicial proceeding.

Romans 2:7, 10, and 13 are not spoken as a *prediction*, as though there actually *will* be people whose works entitle them to eternal life and justification. Instead, these verses state the *principles* on which judgment will be based in God's final assessment of lost men. Each person will get what he deserves. But Paul's doctrine was that no one would gain eternal salvation on the basis of principles like these. In the very next chapter of this epistle (Rom. 3), Paul will demonstrate that very point.

Precisely, then, because men fail to persevere in good works or truly to do God's law, they are utterly shut up to "the righteousness of God which is through faith in Jesus Christ" (Rom. 3:21-26).[19]

Other Pauline Texts

Within the limited scope of this book it is not possible to touch every single passage which at one time or another has been used to prove that Paul treated good works as an "inevitable" outcome of true regeneration. Paul simply did not hold such a view of works, though no writer insists more strongly than he that Christians ought to do them.

Unfortunately, the Apostle has not always been credited with being truly consistent with his fundamental insistence that works have nothing to do with determining a Christian's basic relationship to God. That relationship, in Pauline thought, is founded on pure grace and nothing else.

Often Paul's statements are treated in a very one-dimensional way. Even though every epistle he wrote is addressed to those who have already come to saving faith, his teachings are frequently taken as though he was constantly concerned about the eternal destiny of his readers. But there was no reason why he should have been.

His many direct declarations that his audiences have experienced God's grace show that he was not concerned about this.[20]

Such declarations abound in the Pauline letters, and Ephesians 2 and Titus 3 are merely two of the most notable. Simple statements like, "For you were bought at a price; therefore glorify God in your body and in your spirit, which are God's" (1 Cor 6:20), show exactly what he thought about his readers' relationship to God. There is not even a single place in the Pauline letters where he clearly expresses doubt that his audience is composed of true Christians.

(1) Romans 8:14

So when the Apostle writes, "For as many as are led by the Spirit of God, these are the sons of God" (Rom. 8:14), he is not offering a "test" by which his readers may decide if they are saved or not. His readers possess a faith which "is spoken of throughout the whole world" (Rom. 1:8). They enjoy "peace with God through our Lord Jesus Christ" as well as "access by faith into this grace in which we stand" (Rom. 5:1,2; note the repeated use of "we"). That they could conceivably be unregenerate is the farthest thought from the Apostle's mind.

But for Paul the concept of being a "son of God" involved more than simply being regenerate. As he makes clear in Galatians 4:1-7, a "son" is one who has been granted "adult" status, in contrast to the "child" who is under "guardians and stewards" (Gal. 4:1, 2). This, of course, means that the Christian, as a "son," is free from the law. Thus the statement of Romans 8:14 is identical in force to that of Galatians 5:18: "But if you are led by the Spirit, you are not under the law." The identity between the statements is confirmed also by the reference to "the spirit of bondage" in Romans 8:15.

Consequently, both in Romans 8:14 and Galatians 5:18, Paul is talking about the way in which our freedom from the law is experientially realized. When the Spirit leads the life, there is no more legal bondage. The believer enters into the freedom of real "sonship" to God and that sonship becomes a reality in his day-by-day experience.[21]

(2) Titus 1:16

Nor should a "test" of regeneration be detected in a verse like Titus 1:16: "They profess to know God, but in works they deny Him, being abominable, disobedient, and disqualified for every good work." It is superficial to take the word "deny" as though it meant nothing more than "is not a Christian."

A little reflection will show that there are various ways in which a believer may "deny" God. He may do it *verbally*, as Peter did on the night of our Lord's arrest. But he may also do it *morally* by a lifestyle that contradicts the implications of the truth he professes. How easily this can be done even by a single act that clashes with our Christian profession, every honest Christian ought to be able to know out of his own experience.

Besides, the people Paul has in mind in Titus 1:16 are evidently the same as those of whom he says in verse 13: "Therefore rebuke them sharply, that they may be sound in the faith."

The Greek word for "sound" means to be healthy. Hence, the persons he thinks of are not individuals who are completely outside the Christian faith. Rather, they are people whom he regards as spiritually "sick" and who need a rebuke designed to restore them to good health. So far from showing that Christians cannot drift disastrously from the path of good works, Titus 1:16 shows the reverse!

(3) Romans 1:5 and 16:26

Finally, an expression like "obedience to the faith" (Rom. 1:5; 16:26) has nothing to do with the works that follow salvation. The fact that it does not is widely recognized since the Greek expression is more literally rendered "the obedience of faith." In harmony with one well-known Greek usage of such expressions, the "obedience" in question is "faith" itself.[22]

Naturally, God demands that men place faith in His Son and is angry with them when they do not (John 3:36). Faith is an obedient response to the summons of the Gospel. But the man who exercises faith is reaching out for the unconditional grace of God.

(4) Conclusion

The Apostle Paul remains, therefore, the Apostle of divine grace. No doubt there were those who could twist his teachings into "antinomian" formulations (see Rom. 3:8).

Ironically, the charge of "antinomianism" has frequently been hurled at the book you are now reading. But this theological "swear word" is totally inapplicable here, just as was such a charge in Paul's case.

Paul never allowed such accusations to keep him from teaching the freeness of God's salvation nor did he neglect to call for a lifestyle that was truly responsive to this divine generosity. But the Apostle was also a realist and a pastor who knew only too well the failures to which Christians are prone. Yet he does not for that reason modify his concept of God's saving grace. He simply redoubles his efforts to stir up his fellow Christians to live so that they will honor their true calling (Eph. 4:1).

It may safely be said that no man in Christian history – with the exception of our Lord Himself – ever motivated believers more or threatened them less than did this great servant of Christ. Those who feel unable to inspire lives of obedience apart from questioning the salvation of those whom they seek to exhort have much to learn from Paul.

Postscript:
2 Corinthians 13:5

In the first edition of this book there was no discussion of 2 Corinthians 13:5. This proved to be a significant oversight.   Critics of the book sometimes spoke as though the oversight was due to a reluctance on the author's part to confront this text.[23]

This was not the case. But we did misjudge the role this verse would play in the debate that followed publication of the first edition. The inclusion of 2 Corinthians 13:5 in this second edition is therefore absolutely necessary.

In 2 Corinthians 13, the Apostle Paul is announcing his intention to visit the Corinthian church once more. He writes:

> I have told you before, and foretell as if I were present the second time, and now being absent I write to those who have sinned before, and to all the rest, that if I come again I will not spare – since you seek a proof of Christ speaking in me, who is not weak toward you, but mighty in you. For though He was crucified in weakness, yet He lives by the power of God. For we also are weak in Him, but we shall live with Him by the power of God toward you. Examine yourselves as to whether you are in the faith.   Test yourselves. Do you not know yourselves, that Jesus Christ is in you? – unless indeed you are **disqualified**. But I trust that you will know that we are not **disqualified** (2 Cor. 13:2-6; emphasis added).

Just as with most of the verses already discussed in this chapter, 2 Corinthians 13:5 is often ripped out of its context. Failure to consider the context is almost always a formula for misunderstanding and doctrinal confusion.

(1) The Situation
at Corinth

The situation at Corinth was somewhat different from that which existed when 1 Corinthians was written. Although the church as a whole still had warm regard for Paul (2 Cor. 7:6-16), Paul now had critics and enemies in Corinth. The believers there had listened to these people more than they should have (10:7-12; 11:12-15).

Apparently some of Paul's own converts wondered whether Paul could furnish "proof of Christ speaking" in him (13:3). Paul is now insisting that he will indeed revisit Corinth (see 13:1), though a previously planned trip had been canceled (see 2 Cor. 1:15-2:2). Furthermore, he insists that when he comes his conduct toward them will be marked by the "power of God" (verse 4).

The tone of 2 Corinthians 13:2-4 is both humble and confident. Paul promises not to "spare" those Christians among them who had sinned and had remained unrepentant (see verse 4 and 12:20,21). This implies that Paul will either lead the church to discipline these people or that he himself, through prayer, will deliver them to Satan who will be an instrument for their chastisement. As we saw in the previous chapter, this is what Paul did at a later time with Hymenaeus and Alexander (1 Tim. 1:20).

Paul knows, of course, his own weakness (13:4), yet he has total confidence that his actions at Corinth will be effective because God's power will work through him. The sinning believers will be dealt with in such a way that the Corinthians will get "a proof of Christ speaking in me" (verse 2). In short, Paul says, "we will live with Him [Christ] by the power of God *toward you*" (verse 4, emphasis added).

(2) Paul's Challenge
to the Corinthians

Yet Paul is not so arrogant as to suggest that such

confidence was a special privilege belonging to him alone. True, he knew perfectly well that Christ lived dynamically in him and used him. But could not the Corinthians have the same confidence about themselves?

Of course they could. Provided of course, that their lives did not stand under God's disapproving censure.

So he writes:

> Examine **yourselves** as to whether you are in the faith. Test **yourselves**. Do you not know **yourselves**, that Jesus Christ is in you? – unless indeed you are disqualified (2 Cor. 13:5; emphasis added).

Unfortunately these forceful words are often read as though they challenged the Corinthians to find out whether or not they were *saved.*

This is unthinkable and absurd. After twelve chapters in which the Apostle takes his readers' Christianity for granted, can he *only now* be telling them to make sure they are born again? The question answers itself.

It is impossible to read the first twelve chapters of 2 Corinthians carefully without seeing how frequently the Apostle expresses confidence that his readership is truly Christian. Let us notice a few places where this is true:

> Paul . . . to the church of God which is at Corinth, with all the saints who are in all Achaia (1:1,2).

> Now I trust you will understand to the end . . . that we are your boast as **you also are ours in the day of Jesus Christ** (1:13, 14; emphasis added).

> Now He who establishes us **with you** in Christ . . . (1:21; emphasis added).

> You are our epistle written in our hearts,

> known and read by all men; **clearly you
> are an epistle of Christ**, ministered by
> us, written not with ink but **by the Spirit of
> the living God**, not on tablets of stone but
> **on tablets of flesh**, that is, **of the heart**
> (3:2, 3; emphasis added).
>
> Do not be unequally yoked together with
> unbelievers [the Corinthians are believers!].
> For what fellowship has **righteousness**
> with lawlessness? And what communion has
> **light** with darkness? . . . Or what part has a
> **believer** with an unbeliever? And what
> agreement has **the temple of God** with
> idols? **For you are the temple of the
> living God** (6:14-16; emphasis added).
>
> But as you abound in everything – **in faith**,
> in speech, in knowledge, in all diligence, and
> in your love for us – see that you abound in
> this grace also (8:7; emphasis added).

It is needless to extend this list further. How can
anyone read 2 Corinthians and conclude that Paul
thought his readership needed to find out whether they
were really saved or not?[24] To draw this conclusion from
2 Corinthians 13:5 is to impose on that verse an alien
theology, about which Paul knew nothing at all.

No indeed! Paul is *not* saying, "Examine yourselves to
see whether you are born again, or justified." But he *is*
saying, "Examine yourselves to see if you are *in the faith*."
And this is a different matter.

(3) The Meaning of
"in the Faith"

It is tragic how often a text like this can be read with
preconceived notions about the meanings of certain words
or phrases. Why should anyone assume that the

expression "in the faith" equals "to be a Christian"? On
what grounds is such an assumption based?
What about the same phrase in 1 Corinthians 16:13?
There we read:

> Watch, stand fast **in the faith**, be brave, be
> strong.

Or equally, what about this phrase in Titus 1:13?

> Therefore rebuke them sharply, that they
> may be sound [healthy] **in the faith** [see
> also Titus 2:2].

There are other passages where an equivalent
expression appears. These, too, are helpful:

> . . . strengthening the souls of the disciples,
> exhorting them to continue **in the faith**
> (Acts 14:22).

> Receive one who is weak **in the faith**
> (Rom. 14:1).

> As you therefore have received Christ Jesus
> the Lord, so walk in Him, rooted and built up
> in Him, and established **in the faith** (Col.
> 2:6,7).

> Be sober, be vigilant; for your adversary the
> devil walks about like a roaring lion, seeking
> whom he may devour. Resist him, steadfast
> **in the faith** (1 Pet. 5:8, 9).

In all of the passages we have mentioned, the phrase
"in the faith" relates in some way to our Christian walk or
warfare. The meaning "to be a Christian" is not relevant
in any New Testament passage at all!
We must conclude that the expression "in the faith"
refers instead to the proper sphere of our spiritual

activity. It is the sphere in which we are to "remain," "stand fast," "stand," "resist the devil," and "be spiritually healthy." It is this type of meaning alone that fits the context of 2 Corinthians 13:5.

Paul is quite sure that he himself is "in the faith" in the sense that he is dynamically related to Christ. Christ speaks in him, God's power works through him. He is confident this will be evident when he returns to Corinth.

But the Corinthians can see this in themselves, too, if they will but examine their experience. They can see Jesus Christ living dynamically in themselves as well.

Thus the statement, "Do you not know yourselves, that Jesus Christ is in you?" has no more to do with the question of salvation than do the words "in the faith." What Paul has described of his own experience shows that he is thinking of Jesus Christ being in himself, or in the Corinthians, in a dynamic, active and vital sense.

In the language of the Apostle John this could be expressed in terms of the abiding life, where the disciple is in Christ, and Christ is in the disciple, in a dynamic, fruit-bearing relationship (see John 15:1-8; 14:19-24).[25]

So Paul is saying, "Take a look at yourselves; test yourselves. Can you not see Jesus Christ actively living in you, just as I can see Him in me? Of course you can – unless, however, you are 'disqualified.' "

(4) The Meaning of "Disqualified"

The word "disqualified" is a significant one for Paul. He used it in his first letter to the Corinthian church when he wrote:

> But I discipline my body and bring it into subjection lest when I have preached to others, I myself should become **disqualified** (1 Cor. 9:27; emphasis added).

In this passage, the Apostle has been talking about the

Christian life as a race. He is careful to pursue God's approval in that race so that he will not be "disqualified" from winning the proper reward.

But the Greek word translated "disqualified" basically means "disapproved." In 2 Corinthians 13:5 Paul is telling his Christian readers that as long as they have God's approval on their lives (that is, as long as they are obedient to Him) they will be able to see in their own experience the dynamic reality of Christ living in them.

This could be observable in terms of answered prayer, spiritual blessing, and fruitfulness in the lives of others. Obedient Christians experience such things. Disobedient Christians do not. Obedient believers are living their lives "in the faith." Disobedient believers are cut off from this kind of vital fellowship with Christ.   They may be described as living "according to the flesh" (Rom. 8:13) or as "walking in darkness" (1 John 1:7).

(5) Paul's Concluding Comment

Paul knows he is in fellowship with Christ. "I intend to prove that when I come to Corinth," he says. "But such confidence is not mine alone. It's for you Corinthians too! You can see its reality in yourselves, if you take the trouble to look – unless, after all, God disapproves of your way of life."

Then he adds:

> But I trust that you will know that **we** [the Greek pronoun is emphatic] are not disqualified (13:6).

"When I come to Corinth," says Paul, "I hope to convince you that God's approval rests on me. You can know this about yourselves, and I expect you to know it about me as well!"

Such then was the confident spirit with which the Apostle prepared to go back to Corinth. No doubt he would be horrified to hear his words to his brethren twisted into a call to test their justification by examining their own good works.[26]

Conclusion

Nothing highlights the tragedy of today's evangelical church like the degree to which Paul's teachings are distorted into anti-Pauline thought. After all, it was Paul who wrote:

> But to him **who does not work** but believes on Him who justifies the ungodly, his faith is accounted for righteousness (Rom. 4:5; emphasis added).

But today, many theologians respond to this with a "yes, but . . . " "Yes, but if you don't do works you are not justified at all."[27] In this way, the Pauline declaration is annulled in favor of a faith/works synthesis which is contrary to both the Scriptures and to the doctrine of faith expounded in the Reformation by Calvin and Luther.[28]

It is nothing less than a retreat into the theological darkness that made the Reformation necessary in the first place.   Although those who advocate such doctrine describe it as "orthodox" and "reformational," in reality it is neither.

The evangelical church will have no message for the world if it allows this false doctrine to prevail.

CHAPTER

8

ACTS 2, 19, AND 22:
FAITH AND WATER BAPTISM

The relationship of water baptism to the question of eternal salvation has often been discussed. It is well known that there are many churches where the rite of water baptism is regarded as an indispensable step in Christian conversion. A great deal of commentary literature on the New Testament has been authored by writers who are associated with such churches. It seems necessary to give at least brief consideration to this question here.

John 3:5

In the Gospel of John water baptism is never associated with the offer of eternal life. Yet many have thought that baptism *is* referred to in John 3:5. There Jesus says:

> "Most assuredly, I say to you, unless one is
> born of water and the Spirit, he cannot enter
> the kingdom of God."

The conclusion that the word "water" in this verse refers to "baptism" is not well-founded. If John really had believed that baptism was essential to obtaining eternal life, it is both astounding and inexplicable that he never says so directly. John 3:5 can be adequately interpreted without making the equation "water" = "baptism."

Since the Greek word for "spirit" also meant "wind," it is likely that the expression was originally intended to be understood as "born of water and wind" (see verse 8). In that case, "water" and "wind" are a dual metaphor intended to symbolize the life-giving ministry of God's Spirit. Nicodemus should have been familiar with Old Testament texts which used these images of the Spirit's work. See Isaiah 44:3-5, where the Spirit is compared to life-giving waters poured out from above; and Ezekiel 37:5-10, where He is a life-imparting wind or breath. [1]

This view of the text is defended by the present writer in some detail in an article, "Water and Spirit – John 3:5," *Bibliotheca Sacra*, vol. 135, no. 539, July-September, 1978, pages 206-220. It is sufficient to say here that there is no adequate reason to take Jesus' words as a reference to baptism. The silence of the Fourth Gospel about the spiritual significance of this rite is deafening. [2]

1 Corinthians 1:17

When we turn to the Apostle Paul, he clearly did not view baptism as indispensable to his ministry in the Gospel. In fact, he actually writes:

> For Christ did not send me to baptize, but to
> preach the gospel (1 Cor. 1:17).

It was apparently not Paul's practice even to baptize his own converts (1 Cor. 1:13-16). At the very least, this does not sound like he thought no one could be eternally saved unless they were baptized!

Outside of 1 Corinthians 1 (and 15:29) all the other references to Christian baptism in Paul can be understood as references to baptism by the Holy Spirit. It was *this* baptism which was so vital to Pauline thought. It furnished the grounds on which the believer could be said to be *in* the Body of Christ (see 1 Cor. 12:13).

We should keep in mind that the key word in John's

doctrine of eternal salvation is "life," specifically "eternal
life." For Paul, the key word is "justification." Neither
writer ever associates his basic idea with anything other
than faith. For John, baptism plays no role in obtaining
"life." For Paul, it plays no role in "justification." In fact,
there in no New Testament writer who associates baptism
with either of these issues. The importance of this
observation cannot be overstated.[3]

Acts 2:38

If all this is kept in mind, a new light is cast on the
kind of statement found in Acts 2:38. In that place, Luke
reports the Apostle Peter as saying:

> "Repent, and let every one of you be
> baptized in the name of Jesus Christ for the
> remission of sins; and you shall receive the
> gift of the Holy Spirit."

This text seems clearly to say that the hearers must be
baptized to get their sins forgiven and then, but only then,
will they be given the gift of the Holy Spirit. An effort is
sometimes made to avoid this conclusion by rendering the
word "for" (Greek, *eis*) as "because of," but this procedure
lacks any adequate linguistic basis. The effort to show
that *eis* can mean "because of" has been a failure.[4]
    What the text does *not* say is how the hearers were
"regenerated" and "justified." But the answers of John and
Paul to this question are the only Biblical ones that can be
given: they were justified and regenerated by faith. *There
is nothing in Acts 2:38 to contradict this!*
    On the contrary, Peter concludes his address with the
declaration that "God has made this Jesus, whom you have
crucified, both Lord and Christ" (2:36). His hearers then
reply, "Men and brethren, what shall we do?" (2:37). But
such a reaction presumes their acceptance of Peter's claim
that they have crucified the One who is Lord and Christ. If
this is what they now believed, then they were already

regenerate on John's terms, since John wrote: "Whoever believes that Jesus is the Christ is born of God" (1 John 5:1; see John 20:31).

(1) Justification and Forgiveness

It seems plain that in Peter's audience there were many who accepted the claims of Christ which Peter has presented. These people are enormously convicted of their guilt in the crucifixion and ask what they need to do now. Acts 2:38 is the answer.[5] This verse could never have become a problem to interpreters as long as fundamental Pauline and Johannine truths were kept in mind. Even the reference to the forgiveness of sins is not hard to understand when it is properly considered.

Justification by faith establishes a man's legal standing before his Judge. Forgiveness enables him to have communion with his God.

Even on the level of everyday experience, forgiveness has nothing to do with the courts. A judge does not "forgive" anyone; he finds a man either guilty or innocent. Forgiveness relates instead to personal relationships. Men exclude from their fellowship those whom they refuse to forgive and in turn are excluded by those who will not forgive them.

It may be said then that when a man is *justified* he is given a righteousness which comes from God (Rom. 3:21-26). When he is *regenerated,* he is given the very life of God (John 1:12, 13). But *forgiveness* introduces him to fellowship with the One whose life and righteousness he has been granted through faith.

Not surprisingly, therefore, even those who are both justified and regenerated are taught to seek forgiveness on a regular basis (Luke 11:4; 1 John 1:9). Justification and new birth are irrevocable free gifts (Rom. 5:15-18; 11:29). Fellowship is a conditional privilege (1 John 1:7).

(2) The Special Situation in Acts 2

The situation in Acts 2 is apparently exceptional. It is not repeated in the experience of Gentile converts (Acts 10:43-48). It is probably related to the special guilt of those who had been implicated in the crucifixion. But there is no actual conflict with fundamental Pauline and Johannine truth.

In this special transitional situation, fellowship with God is withheld from these converts until they have been baptized. Following this, the gift of the Spirit is bestowed. But his latter gift was a new one, not given before Pentecost (John 7:39). It is not to be confused with the experience of regeneration which has always been the fundamental requirement for entrance into God's Kingdom (John 3:3). At Pentecost, God gave the Spirit only to those who had entered into fellowship with Himself.[6]

Acts 22:16

The experience just described was Paul's own as well. Clearly Paul came to faith in the Lord Jesus Christ on the road to Damascus (Acts 9:3-5; 22:6-8; 26:12-15). The blazing light in which he met his Savior is probably behind the imagery found in 2 Corinthians 4:6, about the light of the knowledge of Christ shining into our hearts.

If anyone thinks that Paul was not really converted on the Damascus road, this idea would be far-fetched in the extreme. Obviously, from that occasion onward, he was a believer in Jesus, whom he now calls Lord (Acts 22:10).

But he was forgiven three days later! This is plainly indicated by the words of Ananias in Acts 22:16 when he tells Saul:

> "Arise and be baptized, and wash away your sins, calling on the name of the Lord."

Since his faith on the Damascus road had already brought him eternal life and justification, this additional step must have introduced him into the dynamic experience of Spirit-led fellowship with God (see Acts 9:17-20). After three days of fasting and prayer (Acts 9:9, 11), he had found the answer to his question, "What shall I do, Lord?" (Acts 22:10). That answer, his Lord had told him, would be given to him in Damascus (Acts 9:6; 22:10).

It is obvious that this type of experience is completely parallel to the situation in Acts 2:38 – even down to the question, "What shall we do?" It is an experience in which baptism plays an important, but highly exceptional, role. Its terms are never repeated in the book of Acts anywhere on the Gentile mission fields. Neither are such terms presented anywhere else in the epistles of the New Testament.

These terms for fellowship evidently belong to the historic record of God's dealings with the generation of Palestinians who had been exposed to, and had rejected, the ministries of both John the Baptist and Jesus Himself. (See the reference to "this perverse generation" in Acts 2:40.) In both the ministries of John and our Lord, baptism played a significant part (cf. John 4:1, 2). It was suitable for people in this unique historical situation to be required to enter fellowship with God through baptism.[7]

Acts 19:1-7

It is along these lines that we can understand Acts 19:1-7. There we read:

> And it happened . . . that Paul . . . came to Ephesus. And finding some disciples he said to them, "Did you receive the Holy Spirit when you believed?" So they said to him, "We have not so much as heard whether there is a Holy Spirit." And he said to them, "Into what then were you baptized?" So

they said, "Into John's baptism." Then Paul
said, "John indeed baptized with a baptism
of repentance, saying to the people that
they should believe on Him who would come
after him, that is, on Christ Jesus." When
they heard this, they were baptized in the
name of the Lord Jesus. And when Paul laid
hands on them, the Holy Spirit came upon
them, and they spoke with tongues and
prophesied. Now the men were about
twelve in all.

The disciples in this passage, whom Paul met, were
already believers. Paul's question to them makes this
plain: "Did you receive the Holy Spirit when you
believed?" (19:2).   But they were also probably
Palestinians, since they had experienced John's baptism
(19:3). In harmony with the conditions of Acts 2:38, Paul
baptizes them and subsequently imparts to them the Holy
Spirit (19:5, 6).

Non-Palestinians, who had no contact with John's
baptism, are never said in the New Testament to have had
any such experience as this. Of course, the Samaritans of
Acts 8:12-17 were Palestinians!

This is plainly not normative Christian experience.
Normative Christian experience takes the form set forth
in the crucial story of the conversion of Cornelius in Acts
10. There forgiveness and the reception of the Spirit take
place at the moment of faith (10:43, 44). Water baptism
follows and in no way conditions these blessings (10:47,
48).

The situations described in Acts 2, 8, and 19, as well as
Paul's own in 22, are a matter of instructive Biblical
record. But by the time Paul wrote the Epistle to the
Romans, it could be said that all Christians possessed the
Spirit of God (Rom. 8:9; see 1 Cor. 12:13). The transitional
features of the Christian message, which Luke faithfully
reports, are not pertinent today. In fact, they never were
pertinent (even in Acts) on the Gentile mission fields.

Salvation in Luke, Paul and John

This leads to a further important observation. In Luke's writings, and also in Paul's, the term "salvation," or "saved" (in reference to converts to Christianity) is reserved for those who have received *not only* eternal life and justification, *but also* the gift of the Holy Spirit.

Thus the word "saved" is used of Cornelius's experience in direct connection with the gift of the Spirit (Acts 11:14-18). It is applied to the first converts in Acts only when they have been baptized and incorporated into the Church through the bestowal of the Spirit (Acts 2:41, 47). It is the baptism of the Spirit, not new birth alone, that introduces men into the Body of Christ (1 Cor. 12:13). Neither Luke nor Paul ever used the term "saved" of those not yet baptized with the Holy Spirit. In Titus 3:4-7, the outpouring of the Holy Spirit is a prominent part of Paul's description of how God "saved" us.

By contrast, John apparently can refer the term "saved" to those who have simply received eternal life. His use of the expression "saved" is rare, but the examples seem sufficient to prove the point just stated (John 3:17; 5:34; 10:9). It must be kept in mind that those who believed in Jesus during the course of His earthly life received only eternal life. The gift of the Spirit awaited the post-ascension situation (John 7:39).

It follows from this that, in the Johannine sense, the converts of Acts 2 were "saved" *before* they were baptized. That is, they received eternal life the moment they believed in Jesus Christ. But in the Pauline and Lucan sense, they were not "saved" until *after* they were baptized, since only then did they receive the gift of the Spirit.

Even in Paul and Luke's sense of the word, however, all but the first century Palestinians received this "salvation" on the basis of faith alone. But everyone, in all times and places, has received eternal life (and been "saved" in John's sense of the word) by faith and faith alone.

Mark 16:16

If these distinctions are kept in mind, the significance of Mark 16:16 can be properly analyzed. (The grounds for rejecting Mark 16:9-20 as not an authentic part of the original Gospel of Mark are exceedingly insufficient.)[8] In Mark 16:16, Jesus states:

> "He who believes and is baptized will be saved; but he who does not believe will be condemned."

Here the Lord Jesus anticipates Luke and Paul's use of the term "saved." The bestowal of the Spirit, with His accompanying gifts, is clearly in His mind as is proved by verses 17, 18. Thus our Lord speaks here of a "salvation" that involves *not only* eternal life, *but also* the gift of the Spirit.

Naturally His statement is a summary statement. It is designed to cover *all* the post-Pentecostal cases of "salvation." And as exceptional as the situations of Acts 2, 8, and 19 are, they need to be covered by His declaration. So He announces that *everyone* who takes the two steps specified (faith and baptism) will experience the "salvation" He is speaking of.

Yet it has often been noticed that the condemnation in Mark 16:16 rests simply on the failure to believe. This is what we would expect. Eternal life is granted to faith alone (John 3:16; 5:24; etc.), and anyone who has it can never go to hell, whether they are baptized or not. But today, of course, the Holy Spirit is given to every believer, *before* baptism, at the moment of faith in Christ.

1 Peter 3:21

It is not possible here to fully analyze the famous passage in 1 Peter 3:18-22 in which there is a statement that baptism "now saves us" (1 Pet. 3:21). It is enough to say that the emphasis in the context on the Spirit and "spirits" (3:18,19) points strongly to the conclusion that the Apostle has "Spirit baptism" (not water baptism) in mind. For the purposes of this discussion about the rite of baptism with water, 1 Peter 3:21 may be understood as similar to the Pauline and Lucan use of the word "save."9

Forgiveness "in Christ"

Finally, we must say that whenever an individual is baptized by the Holy Spirit and placed "in Christ," he receives at that moment a kind of "positional" forgiveness. This is described in Ephesians 1:7:

> **In Him** we have redemption through His
> blood, the forgiveness of sins, according to
> the riches of His grace (emphasis added).

Naturally, like all else that pertains to our "position" in Christ, this forgiveness is perfect and permanent. But this in no way contradicts the fact that we also experience forgiveness continually at the level of our day-to-day experience.

An unconverted sinner brings years of unforgiven sin to the moment of his conversion. Experientially, he obtains the forgiveness of all those past sins and begins to have fellowship with God. But whenever he commits further sins, he must acknowledge them and seek God's forgiveness (Luke 11:4; 1 John 1:9).

Nevertheless, as a man "in Christ" he has a position that is not altered by his daily experience of failure. In fact, he is seated "in the heavenly places in Christ Jesus" (Eph. 2:6). This superlative relationship to God is never changed by any earthly interruption in his communion with the Father.

The failure to distinguish our permanent experience of forgiveness "in Christ" from our daily experience of cleansing has led to doctrinal confusion. It has actually led some to deny that a believer should ask for forgiveness for his sins, even though Christians are plainly told to do so. After all, the Lord's prayer was given to *disciples*, not to unconverted sinners, and its petitions are to be made *daily* (Luke 11:1-4).

The thought that a believer need never ask God's forgiveness for his sins is an aberration rightly rejected by the Church as a whole. But because a believer possesses eternal life, and is also "in Christ," his sins jeopardize only his fellowship with God day by day. They do not jeopardize his final salvation from hell.

At the level of everyday experience, repentance for our sins is as fitting for us as it was for the converts on the day of Pentecost (Acts 2:38). Only in our case, confession alone (apart from baptism) secures the forgiveness we need (1 John 1:9).

Conclusion

When the New Testament passages on water baptism are studied closely, they in no way conflict with the grace of God. Eternal life is now, and always has been, a gift conditioned by nothing else but faith alone in Christ alone.

CHAPTER

9

ROMANS 8:
WHO ARE THE HEIRS?

Christian heirship is a great New Testament theme.[1] On this subject, the Apostle Paul has made a vital and instructive comment. His statement is found in Romans 8:16, 17, where he writes:

> The Spirit Himself bears witness with our spirit that we are children of God, and if children, then heirs – heirs of God and joint heirs with Christ, if indeed we suffer with Him, that we may also be glorified together.

This declaration is often read as if only one heirship were in view. However, with only a slight alteration of the English punctuation (which is equally permissible in the original Greek), Paul's words may be read as follows:

> . . . and if children, then heirs – heirs of God, and joint heirs with Christ if indeed we suffer with Him, that we may also be glorified together.

Under this reading of the text, there are two forms of heirship. One of these is based on being children of God. The other is based on suffering with Christ. This distinction is crucial for understanding the New Testament teaching on this subject.

Double Heirship

The concept of two kinds of heirship is very natural indeed in the light of Old Testament custom. As is well-known, in a Jewish family all the sons shared equally in their father's inheritance, except for the oldest, or firstborn, son who received a "double portion." That is, he inherited twice as much as the other sons.

Against this background, Paul can be understood as saying that *all* of God's children are heirs, simply because they are children. But those who suffer with Christ have a special "joint heirship" with Christ. It is of great significance that later in this chapter Christ is actually described as "the *firstborn* among many brethren" (8:29).

Naturally, all believers are God's heirs. In the eternal future they will most assuredly inherit all of the blessings which are unconditionally promised to them. Among these is an eternal glory (Rom. 8:30) which is inherent in the resurrection itself. Hence Paul can say, "The body is sown is dishonor, it is raised in glory. It is sown in weakness, it is raised in power" (1 Cor. 15:42, 43). Elsewhere he writes that "we also eagerly wait for the Savior, the Lord Jesus Christ, who will transform our lowly body that it may be conformed to His glorious body" (Phil. 3:20, 21).

Of course, participation in the resurrection is unconditionally guaranteed to every believer in Christ. Jesus' own declaration on this point is definitive:

> "For I have come down from heaven, not to do My own will, but the will of Him who sent Me. This is the will of the Father who sent Me, that of all He has given Me I should lose nothing, but should raise it up at the last day. And this is the will of Him who sent Me, that everyone who sees the Son and believes in Him may have everlasting life; and I will raise him up at the last day" (John 6:38-40).

This passage is emphatic concerning the eternal

security of the believer in Christ. The Lord Jesus Christ has never lost, nor will he ever lose, anyone who has belonged to Him through faith. But equally, though the word "inheritance" is not used here, such words seal the heirship of every Christian. A share in the glorious immortality of the future world is assured to the believer, because Jesus has promised to "raise him up at the last day."

But in Romans 8:17, Paul speaks also of a "co-heirship" that results in "co-glory." This contrast is a bit easier to see in Greek than it is in English.

In the Greek text, Paul juxtaposes two words for "heir," one of which is the simple word for this, and the other a compound word roughly equal to our word "co-heir." Likewise, two other compound words in Paul's text express the thought of "co-suffering" and "co-glorification." As Paul's words make clear, such an heirship is dependent on something more than saving faith. This heirship is contingent on our experience of suffering with Christ.

Romans 8:17 thus confronts us with a double heirship. One of these is for all believers. The other is for believers who suffer in fellowship with Christ.

Co-Reigning with Christ: 2 Timothy 2:12

A similar thought occurs in 2 Timothy 2:12. There the Apostle writes:

"If we endure, we shall also reign with Him."

Here again we meet the thought of suffering. The Greek verb "endure" refers primarily to the endurance of hardships and trials. Moreover, the verb translated "reign with Him" is another compound word like those we met in Romans 8:17. The idea is: "If we endure [suffering], we shall co-reign" (the words "with Him" are implied by the compound verb).

Putting Romans 8:17 together with 2 Timothy 2:12, it is natural to conclude that to be "co-glorified" with Christ

involves "co-reigning" with Him. In other words, the glory
of co-heirship is more than merely participating in the
glorious future world.   It is to share the portion of the
Firstborn Son of God and to *reign* in His Kingdom.[2]

With so glorious a prospect in view, no wonder Paul
aspired to know Christ in "the fellowship of His
sufferings" (Phil. 3:10)!

Service and Co-Reigning: Luke 19:11-27

The connection between fidelity to Christ and the
privilege of sharing the authority of His Kingdom appears
already in the teaching of Jesus Himself. Its most striking
expression is found in the famous parable of the minas (or
pounds) in Luke 19:11-27.

The parable begins with a reference to the inter-advent
period in which we live today as we wait for the Kingdom
of God. Jesus introduces the story with these words:

> "A certain nobleman went into a far country
> to receive for himself a kingdom and to
> return. So he called ten of his servants,
> delivered to them ten minas, and said to
> them, 'Do business till I come.' " (Lk. 19:12,
> 13).

It is easy to see how this relates to contemporary
Christian experience. The minas (a mina was a unit of
money) represent the potential for useful service to Christ
with which every believer is entrusted. His marching
orders are: "Do business till I come."

According to the story which Jesus told, when the
nobleman returned he called each of his servants to
account. This clearly suggests the Judgment Seat of Christ
(Rom. 14:10-12; 2 Cor. 5:9, 11; 1 Cor. 3:11-15; 4:5). The
outcome of this review, as the parable unfolds it, is
varying degrees of authority in the Kingdom. The degree of
authority is based on the measure of each servant's
faithfulness and productivity. Thus one servant receives

authority over ten cities (19:17), another over five (19:19).

Both servants are sharply distinguished from the unproductive servant, who is given no cities to rule and is even deprived of his mina (19:22-24). He thus bears an unmistakable resemblance to a Christian whose works are "burned up" and who "will be saved, yet so as through fire" (1 Cor. 3:15). He had a job to do but he failed to do it. Therefore he is stripped of further responsibility. His mina is taken away.[3]

As emphasized in the previous chapters, it is an illusion to think that every Christian will necessarily persevere in holiness until the end of his life. Such a view finds no support in the New Testament. This is not to say that there *must be* believers who are *totally* without any good word or work whatsoever. The Scriptures do not teach *that* either. Even in 1 Corinthians 3:15 Paul only says, "*If* anyone's work is burned [up] . . . "

So great is the miracle of regeneration that it is virtually unthinkable that it could have no effect at all on what a person says or does over an extended period of time. But God alone may see these effects and the absence of visible works in no way signals that a person is unsaved. However, those who teach that a lifelong perseverance in holiness *must be* the result of true conversion should read their New Testaments again – this time with their eyes open![4]

The "wicked servant" in Jesus' parable failed to engage in his lord's "business" with the mina he had been given. He was not involved in "serving" his master. Whether or not he did other commendable things is not the point of the parable. At least he did not *labor* for his lord. As a result, he does not co-reign with his master over even a single city!

That he also went to hell would be an absurd and unfounded deduction from this parable.

All Christians, then, are heirs of God. But they are not heirs to an equal degree. Their fidelity to the service of Christ, with all its attendant hardships and sufferings, will be the gauge by which that heirship will be measured out to them. Not to teach this simple truth is to deprive believers of one of the most powerful motivations to endurance which the Scriptures contain.

Inheriting the Kingdom: 1 Corinthians 6:9, 10

It is not surprising that those who do not recognize the truths being discussed are impoverished in their ability to motivate both themselves and other believers. Tragically, they often fall back on the technique of questioning the salvation of those whose lives do not meet Biblical standards. But in the process, they undermine the grounds for a believer's assurance and take part (however unwittingly) in the siege of the Gospel.

Paul did not do this, even though he has sometimes been read as if he did. In writing to the Corinthian church he is exasperated that they engage in lawsuits against one another. Of course, he does not question the salvation of those who do this. Instead he says,

> But brother goes to law against brother, and
> that before unbelievers! (1 Cor. 6:6).

The enormous disgrace of this, from Paul's point of view, is that Christians carry Christians to court where unsaved people preside. He denounces this emphatically. His criticism of such conduct continues:

> Now therefore, it is already an utter failure for
> you that you go to law against one another.
> Why do you not rather accept wrong? Why
> do you not rather let yourselves be cheated?
> No, you yourselves do wrong and cheat, and
> you do these things to your brethren!
> (1 Cor. 6:7, 8).

It is precisely at this point that the Apostle turns to the theme of heirship, for he goes on to say:

> Do you not know that the unrighteous will
> not inherit the kingdom of God? Do not be
> deceived. Neither fornicators, nor idolators,
> nor adulterers, nor homosexuals, nor
> sodomites, nor thieves, nor covetous, nor
> drunkards, nor revilers, nor extortioners will
> inherit the kingdom of God (1 Cor. 6:9, 10).

It is as plain as possible that the Apostle intends these words as a warning against the kind of conduct he has been describing in the Corinthian Christians. This is made doubly obvious by the opening statement that "the *unrighteous* will not inherit the kingdom of God." Paul has just charged them with being unrighteous ("you yourselves do wrong"). The connection is clearer in Greek than in English. The word translated "you do wrong" in verse 8 is the Greek verb *adikeite,* and the word for "unrighteous" in verse 9 is a related word, *adikoi.*

What Paul is saying is that the Corinthians are engaged in conduct that can make it impossible to inherit the Kingdom of God. Persistence in this type of behavior will obviously disqualify them from this kind of heirship. No other deduction about Paul's meaning can possibly be fair to the text.

(1) Paul Knows His Readers
Are Saved

But does he thereby call their salvation into question? That is precisely what he does *not* do. Instead he writes:

> And such were some of you. But you were
> washed, but you were sanctified, but you
> were justified in the name of the Lord Jesus
> and by the Spirit of our God (1 Cor. 6:11).

Paul is so far from suggesting to them that perhaps they are not Christians at all, that he even appeals to the fact that they *are!*[5]

Obviously, Paul's catalogue of sins (verses 9, 10) lays heavy stress on immorality. This was also a major problem with the conduct of the Corinthian Christians (see 1 Cor. 5:1-13; 6:12-20). But always he appeals to the certainty that they are Christians, not to any possibility that they are not. So he can say:

> Do you not know that your bodies are members of Christ? Shall I then take the members of Christ and make them members of a harlot? Certainly not! (1 Cor. 6:15).

And he ends the chapter with this appeal:

> Or do you not know that your body is the temple of the Holy Spirit who is in you, whom you have from God, and you are not your own? For you were bought at a price; therefore glorify God in your body and in your spirit, which are God's (6:19, 20).

The Apostle's whole argument for moral behavior by his readers is based on the fact that they are truly God's temple and members of the Body of Christ. They ought to act like what they are.

The widespread idea that Paul actually doubted (or, could doubt) the salvation of his readers on the basis of their behavior is so far from his real perspective that it is incomprehensible how that conclusion could ever be drawn. Such an approach to his statements here about heirship is so hopelessly confused that it manages to miss his point entirely. It draws from these statements an outlook that was totally foreign to Paul's mind.

In speaking of heirship in 1 Corinthians 6:9, 10, the Apostle did not threaten his readers with the loss of eternal salvation. He did not even raise a question about their salvation. But he warned them plainly that, if they did not correct their unrighteous behavior, they confronted a serious consequence. They would not inherit the Kingdom of God.

(2) To Inherit
the Kingdom

Many have assumed that to "inherit" the Kingdom must be the same as "entering" it. But why should such an equation be made?

Even in everyday speech there is a difference between saying, for example, "you will *live* in that house" and "you will *inherit* it." If a wealthy man tells me that I will inherit his house, has he told me nothing more than that I shall reside in it someday? Obviously, he has told me more than that. He has told me that I will *own* that house.

It is extremely careless not to give deeper thought to a significant concept like "inheriting" the Kingdom of God.

In fact, a survey of the Biblical use of the word "to inherit" shows that it is most frequently a synonym for "to possess" or "to own." Equally, the word "inheritance" usually indicates "property" of some sort which a person *owns*. One can find numerous passages where this is true (for example, Gen. 15:7, 8; Ex. 34:9; Lev. 20:24; 25:46; Num. 16:14; 18:21; 26:52-55; Dt. 12:12; Josh. 17:14; Judg. 2:6; Ruth 4:5; 1 Ki. 21:2, 3; Job 42:15; Mark 12:7; Acts 7:5; and many more).

If we keep the idea of "ownership" in mind, obviously the kingdom is not *owned* by those who are only citizens there. Citizens are *subjects* of a kingdom, not its *owners*. Instead, it is the king to whom a kingdom really *belongs*.

It is not surprising, then, to find the future Kingdom of God described as an *inheritance* and as a *possession* of God's Son. So the Psalmist writes:

"Yet I have set My King
On My holy hill of Zion."

"I will declare the decree:
The Lord has said to Me,
'You are My Son,
Today I have begotten
   You.
Ask of Me, and I will give

> You
> The nations for Your
> **inheritance**,
> And the ends of the earth
> for Your **possession**.
> You shall break them with
> a rod of iron;
> You shall dash them in
> pieces like a potter's
> vessel' " (Psalm 2:6-9)

If the future Kingdom of God is seen as the *inheritance* of the King, God's Son, one thing surely follows. Those who also *inherit* that Kingdom must be those who co-reign with the King!

But for this privilege, perseverance in holiness is an indispensable condition. That point is plainly stated in Revelation 2:26, 27:

> "And he who overcomes and keeps My works until the end, to him I will give power over the nations – 'he shall rule them with a rod of iron; they shall be dashed to pieces like the potter's vessels' – as I also received from My Father."

Note that the faithful believer gets precisely what God promised in Psalm 2 as an *inheritance* for His Son! This is co-heirship.

A similar promise is found in Revelation 3:21:

> "To him who overcomes I will grant to sit with Me on My throne, as I also overcame and sat down with My Father on His throne."

It is clear that spiritual victory – and keeping Christ's works until the end – are essential if one wishes to sit with Him on His throne.[6] But could there be any greater challenge to such victory than so splendid an outcome?

In 1 Corinthians 6:9-11, Paul's point is simple and

direct. Unrighteous people of the type he describes can never be co-heirs with Jesus Christ. They can never "inherit" the Kingdom of God. And that is exactly what some of the Corinthians *formerly were.* But now the slate has been wiped clean by the grace of God. "You were washed," "you were sanctified," "you were justified." So Paul is saying, don't become that kind of person again. Don't forfeit the inheritance that otherwise can be yours.

In the light of verse 11, then, it is even astounding that anyone has found a "test" of salvation in this passage. Paul is addressing these who are justified, set apart, and cleansed.

How could he have said it more plainly?

Rewards: A Biblical Motivation

The Pauline passage found in Galatians 5:19-21 is similar to 1 Corinthians 6:9-11. It can be interpreted in exactly the same way. In Galatians, also, the statement about "inheriting" the Kingdom of God occurs in the heart of an exhortation that warns believers against fulfilling "the lust of the flesh" (Gal. 5:16-26). Evidently the Apostle used this truth about the Kingdom as a powerful motivational technique for his Christian brethren. And so should we.[7]

In fact, the Scriptures open up to the faithful believer a marvelous and highly motivating vision of the future. The promises to the "overcomers" in Revelation 2 and 3 are a significant part of this vision.

For example, it is in Revelation 2 that we meet the mysterious tree of life:

> To him who overcomes I will give to eat from the tree of life, which is in the midst of the Paradise of God (Rev. 2:7).

Clearly this is a *reward* for the "overcomer." A person who has Christ within him will not need a physical tree, however wonderful, to sustain his spiritual life. Yet obviously such a tree could offer some kind of superlative enrichment of one's experience in the Kingdom of God. But whatever the tree of life has to impart to those who are granted the right to partake of it, this must be truly worth striving for.

It seems evident that in exploring the territory set before us in these promises to the "overcomers," we come close to realities impossible to describe precisely to men still in their earthbound flesh. Paul had once been exposed to "inexpressible words" which he was not allowed to repeat (2 Cor. 12:4). The vagueness surrounding the promise of the tree of life is an example of the deliberate indefiniteness of the rewards mentioned in Revelation 2 and 3. Almost all of the other promises to "overcomers" have something of the same undefined, but spiritual, character.

Yet this very vagueness makes the rewards more tantalizing and alluring. Motivation through rewards is found frequently in the New Testament.

Postscript: Revelation 2:11 and 3:5

However, there are two promises to "overcomers" which are often taken as a threat to the security of the believer. These are:

> He who overcomes shall not be hurt by the second death (Rev. 2:11).

> He who overcomes shall be clothed in white garments, and **I will not blot out his name from the Book of Life;** but I will confess his name before My Father and before His angels (Rev. 3:5; emphasis added).

Both promises are best understood as examples of "litotes." "Litotes" is the name for a figure of speech in which a positive idea is stated by negating its opposite. We use it all the time in everyday speech.

Some examples may help: "that test was no snap" (meaning, "the test was hard"); "this suit sure isn't a bargain (= "this suit's expensive"); "he couldn't solve it to save his life" (= "he's completely stumped"); "you aren't the first to make that mistake" (= "lots of people have made the mistake"); Hebrews 6:9 – "God is not unjust to forget your work . . . "(in context = "God will remember and stand by you").

One frequent feature of litotes is that the negative statement is so obviously true ("God is not unjust") or so clearly exaggerated ("you are not the first") that the positive idea easily suggests itself ("God is fair" or "many others preceded you"). Such is the case in Revelation 2:11 and 3:5.

The first century hearer or reader of Revelation, who knew John's doctrine, *knew* that no Christian was in danger of the second death or of having his name erased from the Book of Life (see John 4:13, 14; 5:24; 6:37-40; etc.). Thus it was self-evident (obviously true) that a Christian would "not be hurt by the second death" or that Christ would "not blot out his name from the Book of Life." Litotes is thus suggested. A positive idea is implied.

What is the positive idea implied in 2:11? Verse 10 gives us some direction: "Be faithful until death, and I will give you *the crown of life*" (emphasis added).   The overcomer will have a superlative, "crowning" experience of life in the age to come. So much so, in fact, that to say he is not "hurt by the second death" is an enormous understatement. Life *far beyond* the reach of the second death is implied.[8] To say it another way (using litotes), the overcomer is certainly *not* among those who are "saved . . . through fire" (2 Cor. 3:15)!

What is the positive idea implied in 3:5? This time direction is offered by the closing words of the verse: "but I will confess his name before My Father and before His angels." The overcomer will possess a glorious name which is highly honored before God and the angels. To say that the Lord will "not blot out his name from the Book of Life" is an enormous understatement. A name *far above* such disgrace as that is implied.[9] To say it another way (again using litotes), God will certainly *not* "blot out the remembrance" of the overcomer "from under heaven" (cf. Ex. 17:14)!

Finally, let it be observed that the litotes in Revelation 2:11 and 3:5 fit the indefinite and spiritual character of all the promises to "overcomers." In each of these promises we catch only a glimpse of the reward that is offered. Each reward is deeply attractive. The inspired text deliberately leaves us wanting to know more.

Conclusion

One further point needs to be made. 1 John 5:4, 5 cannot be used to define the term "overcomer" in Revelation 2 and 3. The content and thrust of each context are widely different. 1 John 5:4, 5 declare that faith in Christ is itself a victory over the world which lies under Satanic delusion (1 John 5:18; compare 2 Cor. 4:3-6). In that sense all believers are "overcomers." But Revelation 2 and 3 are talking about the struggles and snares faced by the Christians in the various churches of Asia. It is by no means declared that all of them will "overcome." A careful reading of the seven letters will show that the opposite is suggested.

As one writer has correctly pointed out in connection with the promises to the "overcomers": "A command that everyone keeps is superfluous, and a reward that everyone receives for a virtue everyone has is nonsense."[10]

It is utterly unbiblical to claim that fidelity, even to the point of martyrdom (Rev. 2:10), and dedication to resist the spiritual corruption and decline all around us (Rev. 2:5, 15, 16; 3:3, 4; etc.) are "inevitable" results of simply being a true Christian. Those who claim this are looking at life from an ivory tower that is totally divorced from the down-to-earth realism of the New Testament writers. If we refuse to face the possibility of failure, we in fact prepare the way for failure.

"Therefore let him who thinks he stands take heed lest

he fall" (1 Cor. 10:12).

The price of spiritual victory is high. Let no one be under any delusion about that. But the price is well worth paying.   Every   sacrifice   will   be   more   than   amply rewarded. And at the end of the path lies co-heirship with the King of kings.[11]

CHAPTER

10

GRACE TRIUMPHANT

Perhaps it would be well to restate the thesis of this book as clearly as possible.

Basically we insist that *the New Testament Gospel offers the assurance of eternal life to all who believe in Christ for that life. The assurance of the believer rests squarely on the Biblical promises in which this offer is made, and on nothing else.*

We emphatically reject the claim that a believer must find his assurance in his works. This idea is a grave and fundamental theological error. It is an error that goes right to the heart of the nature of the Gospel proclamation. It seriously distorts that proclamation and creates in its place a new kind of message that would have been unrecognizable to the New Testament writers.

In taking this stance, we also agree with John Calvin's insistence that assurance is part and parcel of what it means to believe in Christ.[1] We fully approve of this statement by him:

> In short, no man is truly a believer, unless he be firmly persuaded, that God is a propitious and benevolent Father to him . . . unless he depend on the promises of the Divine benevolence to him, and feel an undoubted expectation of salvation (*Institutes* III.II.16).

Modern teachers and theologians who separate faith

and assurance have abolished the Biblical concept of faith and denied the Biblical grounds for assurance. Their concept of saving faith is neither orthodox nor reformational. The "gospel" that results from such theology cannot avoid the anathema of Galatians 1:8, 9. This is a serious charge. But it is made thoughtfully and with much grief that it is necessary to make it at all.

Preachers and theologians cannot have it both ways. Either a man can be perfectly sure that he is born again and going to heaven at the moment he believes in Christ, or he cannot. If works must verify a man's faith, then he cannot. It can even be argued that he can *never* be sure until he meets God. But this is not what the New Testament teaches. It is therefore a falsehood and subversive of Biblical truth.

Let it be said clearly: the point of this book is *not* to argue that Christians should not take sin seriously. Of course they should. In fact they should cast themselves on the strength and power of God to avoid it. And spiritual victory, along with rich fellowship with the Father and the Son, is marvelously available to all who do so.

So this book is not written to justify the sin and failure that so often occur in the Christian Church. This book is an attempt to face that failure honestly, just as the New Testament writers did. But there is no attempt to excuse it.

This book *is* about the Gospel. And it is also about a satanic siege of the Gospel in which the simplicity, clarity, and freeness of the Gospel message have come under assault. It is an effort to focus the Church on the issues which are at stake in this attack. It is the prayer of the writer that many will be aroused to stand firmly for the true grace of God.

Grim as the battle is, however, its outcome is not in doubt. Grace will be triumphant. No matter how much confusion the Enemy of souls is able to inject into professing Christendom, there will always be those who understand and proclaim God's free gift of eternal life. The Bible is clear about this gift and God's message has never lacked messengers.

But grace will be triumphant in another way as well. Someday the failures now so painfully evident among those who trust Christ will be forever gone. Everyone who has ever accepted God's gracious salvation will one day be conformed to the image of His Son (Romans 8:29) and will enter the eternal world totally free from the least trace of sin. No doubt not all of them will have attained to "co-heirship" with Jesus Christ. But all of them will be among history's immortals.

It is one measure of the triumph of God's grace that the Apostle John can describe the eternal state with these words:

> But the cowardly, unbelieving, abominable, murderers, sexually immoral, sorcerers, idolaters, and all liars shall have their part in the lake which burns with fire and brimstone, which is the second death (Rev. 21:8).

This is not, of course, salvation by works after all! It is rather a declaration that in the new heavens and the new earth (see Rev. 21:1), there are no more cowards, no more idolaters, no more liars – except those who have been consigned to the lake of fire.

But what about born again believers who have done these things? To be specific, what about wise Solomon who ended his life in spiritual departure from his God and with idolatry (1 Kings 11:1-10)? The answer is that all born again people will be in the presence of God as citizens of the eternal world. And whatever their failures on earth may have been, these are gone. If they had been liars, they are liars no more. If idolaters, they are idolaters no more. Now they are immortal and sinless. They are conformed to the image of God's Son.

How did they come to this place? By the grace of God. For even when God's people fail Him, He does not fail them. He always keeps His Word. In that sense, too, grace will be triumphant.

No wonder that it is with direct reference to God's faithfulness that the great Apostle of grace declares:

> "Indeed, let God be true but every man a liar"
> (Rom. 3:4).

And again, in 2 Timothy 2:13, he wrote:

> If we are faithless, He remains faithful; He
> cannot deny Himself.

POSTSCRIPT:
THE SUFFICIENCY OF THE CROSS

False doctrine in today's church often begins like this: "If he is *really* saved, he will . . . "

The ways of completing this statement are extremely numerous:

> " . . . he will be baptized."
> " . . . he will never deny the faith."
> " . . . he will persevere in good works."
> " . . . he will never commit murder."

And so on. The list could be lengthened greatly.

What is wrong with all these statements?

First, they are *man's* statements, not *God's*. And no matter how often they are repeated, they are unsupported by the Bible. One of the aims of this book has been to show that there are no Scriptural proofs for such claims.

But second, these statements are an insult to the cross of Christ. As tests of our salvation, what they basically imply is this:

> "You cannot find peace or assurance by
> looking to Christ and His cross alone."

Without exception these claims focus a person's heart on what *he* does, or does not, *do*. By so much they tell us that it is dangerous – even wrong – to trust completely in what Christ *has done for us* in dying for all our sins (1 John 2:2; John 1:29). Such claims tell us that unless *we* do something, we are not saved.

No doubt the statements we are criticizing are often made sincerely. Both theologians and lay people often think that these "provisos" are needed to protect God's reputation from dishonor and disgrace. They think that God is defamed if He is identified with people who fail in these ways.

But they should read their Bibles more carefully. God's name is forever associated with the nation of Israel, whose failures and rebellion are recorded in Scripture with total frankness. Moreover, Israel's greatest king, David, committed adultery and murder, and her wisest king, Solomon, compromised with idolatry. But while such failures in His people give God's enemies a chance to blaspheme Him, they do not in any real way diminish His holiness and His glory. The cross of Christ remains the ultimate vindication of the holiness and glory of God the Father, who "sent His Son to be the propitiation for our sins" (1 John 4:10).

We must stop trying to defend God. He does this far better than we can. And in our feeble efforts to maintain His reputation for holiness, we can wind up slandering the cross on which His Son died for our sins.

Either a man can look to the cross and find peace by believing, or he cannot. If he must watch his subsequent performance, then he cannot.

There is no escape from this conclusion. If I cannot trust *completely* in Christ and what *He did* on the cross, then the cross can give no peace about my eternal destiny. I must trust, at least partly, in what *I do* for Him.

The truth that the believer must focus on Christ and His sacrifice is the most profound insight of the Reformation. Yet this insight has been lost by many Protestant churches in the world today as their theology sinks backward towards the old Roman Catholic formulation that faith cannot save apart from works of love. We need to hear again the words of Luther, writing in his famous commentary on Galatians – words which are as relevant today as when they were first penned:

Now the truth of the Gospel is, that our righteousness cometh by faith alone, without the works of the law. The corruption or falsehood of the Gospel is, that we are justified by faith, but not without the works of the law. With this condition annexed, the false apostles preached the Gospel. Even so do our sophisters and Papists at this day. For they say that we must believe in Christ, and that faith is the foundation of our salvation: but it justifieth not, except it be furnished with charity [=love]. This is not the truth of the Gospel, but falsehood and dissimulation. But the true Gospel indeed is, that works of charity [love] are not the ornament or perfection of faith: but that faith of itself is God's gift and God's work in our hearts, which therefore justifieth us, because it apprehendeth Christ our redeemer. Man's reason hath the law for his object, thus thinking with itself: This I have done, this I have not done. But faith being in her own proper office, hath no other object but Jesus Christ the Son of God, delivered to death for the sins of the whole world. It looketh not to charity [love]; it saith not: What have I done? What have I offended? What have I deserved? But [it saith]: What hath Christ done? What hath he deserved? Here the truth of the Gospel answereth thee: He hath redeemed thee from sin, from the devil, and from eternal death. Faith therefore acknowledgeth that in this one person, Jesus Christ, it hath forgiveness of sins and eternal life. *He that turneth his eyes away from this object, hath no true faith,* but a phantasy and a vain opinion, and turneth his eyes from the promise to the law, which terrifieth and driveth to desperation (italics added).[1]

And that, gracious reader, is what this book has been all about. So what about you? Where do you look for peace and assurance of salvation? Are you asking, "Have I done enough to prove I am saved?" Or is the question instead, "Has Christ done enough on the cross to save me, whatever my faults and failures are or may become?" Does your entire hope for heaven rest on what *He has done* and *not at all* on what you can, have, or will, do? If your answer to this last question is yes, then – clearly! – you have believed the Gospel and you already know that your eternal destiny is secure.

Let it be said plainly: any system of doctrine that forbids us to find complete peace by simply looking to God's Son, who was lifted up for us on the cross, can by no means claim to be the true Gospel. But if it is not, then it must be a false gospel and must stand under the anathema Paul pronounced in Galatians 1.

Yet despite the widespread denial of the Bible's simple message of faith, the truth of God stands firm. The words of Jesus remain dependable in all their wondrous simplicity:

> And as Moses lifted up the serpent in the wilderness, even so must the Son of Man be lifted up, that whoever believes in Him should not perish but have everlasting life (John 3:14, 15).

Needless to say, so superb a message has left its unmistakable imprint on Christian hymnology:

> Nothing in my hand I bring,
>   Simply to Thy cross I cling,
> Naked come to Thee for dress;
>   Helpless look to Thee for grace;
> Foul, I to the fountain fly,
>   Wash me, Savior, or I die![2]

> * * *

> Just as I am, without one plea,
>   But that Thy blood was shed for me,

And that Thou bidd'st me come to Thee,
  O Lamb of God, I come! I come!

Just as I am, Thou wilt receive,
  Wilt welcome, pardon, cleanse, relieve;
Because Thy promise I believe,
  O Lamb of God, I come! I come![3]

* * *

My faith has found a resting place,
  Not in device nor creed,
I trust the Everliving One,
  His wounds for me shall plead.

My heart is leaning on the Word,
  The written Word of God,
Salvation by my Savior's name,
  Salvation through His blood.

I need no other argument,
  I need no other plea,
It is enough that Jesus died,
  And that He died for me.[4]

May the Lord Jesus revive His church again to exalt
His marvelous grace.
  Thanks be unto God for His unspeakable gift!
                              –2 Corinthians 9:15 (KJV)

EPILOGUE

When Jimmy got home from work that night, he got out his Bible and began to read the Gospel of John.

Pretty soon he had read verses like John 1:12; 3:16; 4:10; and 5:24. As he did so, his assurance and joy began to return.

"I sure don't know where Bill is coming from," he said to himself, "but I know what these verses are saying. I know I have believed, so I know I have everlasting life!"

With the return of joy came a renewed desire to please God, not to prove he was saved, but out of gratitude for God's goodness.

A casualty in the siege of the Gospel? Yes, for a while. But it was only a surface wound. And the curative powers of God's Word are magnificent.

What Jimmy needs now is a church that preaches a clear Gospel and that expounds God's truth faithfully and well.

Meanwhile, he really *is* saved and God's faithfulness will not fail him.

The outlook is good. Jimmy will be all right.

ENDNOTES

ABBREVIATIONS

AB   The Anchor Bible

BGD   *A Greek-English Lexicon of the New Testament and Other Early Christian Literature*, 2nd edition Revised and Augmented by F. Wilbur Gingrich and Frederick W. Danker from Walter Bauer's Fifth Edition, 1958 (Chicago: University of Chicago Press, 1979).

BNTC   Black's New Testament Commentaries

BSC   Bible Study Commentary

CGNT   Cambridge Greek New Testament

Comm.   Stands exclusively for the commentaries of John Calvin which are always quoted from the series *Calvin's Commentaries*, ed. David W. Torrance and Thomas F. Torrance (Grand Rapids: Eerdmans, various dates).

Herm   Hermeneia – A Critical and Historical Commentary on the Bible.

HNTC   Harper's New Testament Commentaries

ICC   International Critical Commentary

Institutes   John Calvin's *Institutes of the Christian Religion*, always quoted from the 2 vol. translation by John Allen (Philadelphia: Westminster Press, 1935).

MNTC   Moffatt New Testament Commentary

NIC   New International Commentary

NIGNTC   New International Greek New Testament Commentary

TNTC   Tyndale New Testament Commentaries

WBC   Word Biblical Commentaries

WC   Westminster Commentaries

Chapter 1

[1]Gerstner admits the accuracy of the last two of our three statements as expressions of Reformed thought. "We will grant that is an accurate statement of our contention." But he goes on to argue that I really do not understand what Reformed theology is saying, since (he claims) I think that "works are some sort of addendum, something beyond faith itself" in Reformed teaching. But Gerstner did not read the page from which he quotes carefully enough. In some forms of theology works *are* an addendum to faith. But immediately after I point this out (*TGUS*[1], p. 4), I have Reformed doctrine in mind when I write: "Often, in fact, a distinction is drawn between the kind of faith which saves and the kind which does not. But the kind of faith which *does* save is always seen to be the kind that results in some form of overt obedience. . . 'Saving' faith has thus been subtly redefined in terms of its fruit." My charge against Reformed theology is that its insistence on the doctrine of perseverance requires it to redefine "saving faith" in a way that abandons the Biblical and reformational teaching about faith and assurance. Is this not precisely what Gerstner in effect admits when he writes: "Lordship teaching does not 'add works', as if faith were not sufficient. *The 'works' are part of the definition of faith*" (italics added). Neither the Bible nor the great Reformers (Calvin, Luther, Melanchthon) know anything of a definition of faith like this. See John H. Gerstner, *Wrongly Dividing the Word of Truth: A Critique of Dispensationalism* (Brentwood, TN: Wolgemuth and Hyatt, 1991), pp. 225-226 and 257.

[2]The results of this redefinition of saving faith are a theological disaster. So Gerstner can say this: "The question is not whether good works are necessary. As the inevitable outworking of saving faith, they are necessary for salvation" (p. 210). On the same page, two sentences earlier he had written, "Thus good works may be said to be *a condition for obtaining salvation* in that they inevitably accompany genuine faith" (italics added). Calvin would surely have recoiled at such statements. Let us hear Calvin's own words: "The sophists who amuse and delight themselves with perversion of Scripture and vain cavils, think they have found a most excellent subterfuge, when they explain *works* in these passages, to mean those which men yet unregenerate perform without the grace of Christ, merely through the unassisted efforts of their own free-will; and deny that they relate to spiritual works. Thus, according to them, a man is justified both by faith and by works, only the works are not properly his own, but the gifts of Christ and the fruits of regeneration. For they say that Paul spoke in this manner, only that the Jews, who relied on their own strength, might be convinced of their folly in arrogating righteousness to themselves, whereas it is conferred on us solely by the Spirit of Christ, not by any exertion properly our own. But they do not observe, that in the contrast of legal and evangelical righteousness, which Paul introduces in another place, all works are excluded, by what title soever they may be distinguished. For he teaches that this is the righteousness of the law, that he who has fulfilled the command of the law shall obtain salvation; but that the righteousness of faith consists in believing that Christ has died and is risen again. Besides, we shall see, as we proceed, in its proper place, that sanctification and righteousness are *separate blessings of Christ* (italics added). Whence it follows, that even spiritual works are not taken into the account, when the power of justifying is attributed to faith. And the assertion of Paul, in the place just cited, that Abraham has not whereof to glory before God, since he was not justified by works, ought not to be restricted to any literal appearance or external display of virtue, or to any efforts of free-will; but though the life of the patriarch was spiritual, and almost angelic, yet his works did not possess sufficient merit to justify him before God." Calvin, *Institutes* III.xi.14.

It is clear that the theology of Gerstner is light-years removed from that of John Calvin. For Calvin, in no sense are "works" (either before or after justification) a "condition for salvation." At its essential core, Gerstner's soteriology is not reformational, but Roman Catholic.

[3]The sequel and companion volume to *The Gospel Under Siege* is my book *Grace in Eclipse: A Study on Eternal Rewards*, 2nd ed. (Dallas: Redencion Viva, 1987). For an excellent treatment of the role of rewards in Christian motivation, see Charles Stanley, *Eternal Security: Can You Be Sure?* (Nashville: Oliver Nelson, 1990), pp. 106-130.

Chapter 2

[1]Dabney states the Reformed view with bold (and tragic) candor. He writes: "A second objection [to the Plymouth Brethren view of assurance] is: Consciousness reveals to me precisely my own subjective mental states if it is clear in its revelations. Is not that correct? But the question I have to settle, in order to entitle myself to the assurance of hope, is this, viz.: Whether this my subjective mental state is the faith which saves; for notoriously there is a temporary faith simulating the real. That act of self-consciousness does not decide this question; it only presents *the thing to be compared*, namely, my subjective state. The standard of comparison is the Word. When I think I believe, I am but conscious of exercising *what I think is faith*. That is all which this immediate act of self-consciousness contains. *Whether I think right*, in thinking that to be true faith of which I am conscious, is a question of comparison *to be settled by the Word*, which describes the true exercise." See *Discussions by Robert L. Dabney*, vol. 1: *Theological and Evangelical*, ed. C. R. Vaughn (Richmond, VA: Presbyterian Committee of Publication, 1890), p. 225 (italics in Dabney).

In the statements just quoted Dabney means, of course, that what he *thinks* may be saving faith must be tested by his conformity to the moral and ethical demands of God's Word. The tragic result of this process is that a man must look elsewhere than at Christ and the cross to find personal assurance of salvation.

Dabney states this clearly (p. 226): "The necessary object of faith is a gracious Saviour; while my soul looks at him, faith may be in exercise. I wish to inspect my consciousness of the faith exercise. Then the affection of which I was conscious becomes the object; *the gracious Saviour ceases to be, for the time, the object of attention* [italics added], and the affection, as the present exercise, vanishes under inspection. How clear is it, hence, that the thing whose nature I really judge is the *remembrance* [italics his] of my consciousness? If then the consciousness was to any degree indistinct or its remembrance dim, trustworthy inspection cannot take place. But I proved in the previous paragraph the necessity of this inspection or self-acquaintance in order to the assurance of hope. What follows? I infer, with Chalmers, that imperfect but genuine believers may often have actings of faith of such kind that their self-consciousness of them does not ground an assurance of hope; and thence that it is useful and important for their peace to compare with scripture their remembered consciousness of *other gracious actings* [italics added], which, the word tells them, are also marks of a saved state. 'In the mouth of two or three witnesses' they gain the solid advantage of concurrent evidences."

These words reveal starkly how fully Dabney has surrendered the Reformers' view of assurance as being *of the essence of* (inseparable from) saving faith itself.

Indeed, Dabney even admits that this is the case. He says (p. 173): "The source of this [Plymouth Brethren] error is no doubt that doctrine concerning faith which the first Reformers, as Luther and Calvin, were led to adopt from their opposition to the hateful and tyrannical teachings of Rome. This mother of abominations denies to Christians all true assurance of hope, teaching that it is neither edifying nor attainable . . . These noble Reformers, seeing the bondage and misery imposed by this teaching upon sincere souls, *flew to the opposite extreme* [italics added], and (to use the language of theology) asserted that the assurance of hope is of the essence of saving faith."

Subsequently, in the second of two treatises called "Theology of the Plymouth Brethren," he responds to a correspondent (identified as M.N.) who had objected to Calvin being charged with the "error" Dabney had ascribed to him. So Dabney writes (p. 216): "Now, I assert that Calvin. . . was incautious enough to fall into the erroneous statement, that no faith was a living faith which did not include essentially both the assurance of faith and the assurance of hope. He is not satisfied that even the weak, new believer shall say, 'I believe, with head and heart both, that Christ saves *all who truly come to him* [italics his], and I accordingly try to trust him alone for my salvation, and so far as I have any hope, rest it on him alone'. He requires every one to say, in substance, I believe fully that Christ *has saved me* [italics his]. Amidst all Calvin's verbal variations, this is always his meaning; for he is *consistent in his error* [italics added]. What else is the meaning of that definition which M.N. himself quotes from the *Institutes*: 'Our steady and certain knowledge of the divine benevolence *toward us*' [italics his]. But I will show, beyond all dispute, that the theological 'Homer nodded', not once, but all the time, on this point. See then *Institutes* Book III., Chap. II., Sec. 16. 'In short, no man is truly a believer, unless he be firmly persuaded that God is a propitious and benevolent Father *to him*, . . . [italics and ellipsis his] and feel an undoubted expectation of salvation.' "

We may conclude our quotation of Dabney with this telltale observation made by him (p. 215): ". . . I assert: 1. That Calvin and Dr. Malan, and the Plymouth Brethren, hold a definition of the nature or essence of saving faith which is, in one respect, contrary to the Westminster Confession and to the Scriptures, as well as to the great body of the confessions of the Presbyterian Churches, and of their divines since Calvin's day. I said, by way of apology for the earliest Reformers, and most notably, Luther and Calvin, that they were betrayed into this partial error by a praiseworthy zeal against the opposite and mischievous error of Rome, who seeks to hold believers always in doubt of their salvation. . . Now I give this explanation of Calvin's partial error to save his credit. M.N. will not have it so; then he will needs have his admired leader discredited, for as sure as truth is history, Luther and Calvin did fall into this error, which the Reformed churches, led by the Westminster Confession, have since corrected."

Dabney's articles, from which we have cited, are well worth reading in their entirety. But we have quoted enough to show the following: (1) On the subject of faith and assurance, Calvin is at odds with Reformed theology and with the Westminster Confession; (2) since, for Dabney, Calvin's error was an overreaction against Roman Catholicism, the correction of this error by the Reformed churches amounts to a retreat in the direction of Catholic theology.

More recent historical studies have strongly reaffirmed the difference between Calvin and post-Calvin "Calvinism" in the area of faith and assurance. See A. N. S. Lane, "Calvin's Doctrine of Assurance," *Vox Evangelica* 11(1979):32-54; R. T. Kendall, *Calvin and English Calvinism to 1649* (Oxford: University Press, 1979); and M. Charles Bell, *Calvin and Scottish Theology: The Doctrine of Assurance* (Edinburgh: The Handsel Press, 1985).

To the best of this writer's knowledge, none of today's leading Reformed theologians, who are critical of *The Gospel Under Siege*, have yet admitted in print the facts reviewed in this footnote. Why not?

[2]The Greek tenses in John 4:10 would permit the following interpretation of the NKJV rendering:

> "If you [now] knew the gift of God, and who it is who says to you, 'Give Me
> a drink', you would [already] have asked Him, and He would [already] have
> given you living water".

This understanding clarifies the conclusion of the story. As I have pointed out in *Absolutely Free! A Biblical Reply to Lordship Salvation* (Dallas: Redencion Viva, 1989), pp. 41-42: The "water of life" is the life-begetting truth that "Jesus is the Christ." She asked Him for this (v. 25) and He gave it to her (v. 26). Her statement in verse 26 is clearly a functional question which implies: "Are you perhaps the Messiah?" When Jesus replied that He was, her reception of this great truth in faith – that is, her persuasion that it was true – brought salvation. Once she knew this truth by faith (see John 20:31; 1 John 5:1), the asking and giving had already occurred.

[3]In what must be a classic case of reading one's own ideas into a text, John MacArthur writes about the Israelites bitten by fiery serpents (Numbers 21) as

follows: "In order to look at the bronze snake on the pole, *they had to drag themselves* [italics added] to where they could see it. They were in no position to glance flippantly at the pole and then proceed with lives of rebellion"! But this is a transparent effort to extract (non-existent) support from the Old Testament text for MacArthur's own doctrine of "hard believism" (="lordship salvation"). Clearly the story in Numbers glorifies God's grace by the extreme simplicity of the divine solution to the Israelites' desperate need. So too, faith is "looking to" Jesus for our salvation and is God's simple solution to man's urgent spiritual need. MacArthur's "eisegesis" of the Numbers story is appalling. See John F. MacArthur, *The Gospel According to Jesus: What Does Jesus Mean When He Says "Follow Me"* (Grand Rapids: Zondervan Publishing House, 1988), p. 46.

[4]Gerstner rejects the universal scope of John 3:16 due to his doctrine of limited atonement. His statements about it are both bald and horrifying. He writes that this verse "is supposed to teach that God so loved everyone in the world that He gave His only Son to provide them an opportunity to be saved by faith. What is wrong with this interpretation? First, such a love on God's part, so far from being love, would be *a refinement of cruelty* [italics added]. As we have seen, offering a gift of life to a spiritual corpse, a brilliant sunset to a blind man, and a reward to a legless cripple if only he will come and get it, are *horrible mockeries*" (italics added). See Gerstner, p. 124.

As I pointed out in my review of Gerstner's book in the GES Journal, we might more readily say that if God had created immortal human beings for whom He made no saving provision so that they could escape eternal damnation, that *this* would be "a refinement of cruelty"! See my "Calvinism Ex Cathedra: A Review of John H. Gerstner's *Wrongly Dividing the Word of Truth: A Critique of Dispensationalism*," *Journal of the Grace Evangelical Society* 4(2,1991):66-67.

[5]Calvin's own definition of faith is outstanding and justly famous. It is notably free of the complications introduced by Reformed and 'lordship' theologians. Calvin writes:

> Now, we shall have a complete definition of faith, if we say, that it is a steady and certain knowledge of the Divine benevolence toward us, which, being *founded on the truth of the gratuitous promise in Christ*, is both revealed to our minds and confirmed to our hearts, by the Holy Spirit (*Institutes* III.ii.7; italics added).

R. T. Kendall, p. 19, neatly summarizes Calvin's view of faith: "The position which Calvin wants pre-eminently to establish (and fundamentally assumes) is that faith is *knowledge*. Calvin notes some biblical synonyms for faith, all simple nouns, such as 'recognition' (*agnitio*) and 'knowledge' (*scientia*). He describes faith as illumination (*illuminatio*), knowledge as opposed to the submission of our feeling (*cognitio, non sensus nostri submissio*), certainty (*certitudino*), a firm conviction (*solida persuasio*), assurance (*securitas*), firm assurance (*solida securitas*), and full assurance (*plena securitas*)" (italics all in Kendall). For the terms Kendall attributes to Calvin, he notes the following references: *Institutes* III with these chapters and sections: ii.14; i.4; ii.2; ii.6; ii.16(three times); ii.22.

Kendall (pp. 19-20) proceeds: "What stands out in these descriptions is the given, intellectual, passive, and assuring nature of faith. What is absent is a need for gathering faith, voluntarism, faith as man's act, and faith that must await experimental knowledge to verify its presence. Faith is 'something merely passive, bringing nothing of ours to the recovering of God's favour but receiving from Christ that which we lack.' It is but the 'instrument (*instrumentum*) for receiving righteousness', a 'kind of vessel' (*quasi vas*), which transmits the knowledge of our justification: 'a passive work, so to say, to which no reward can be paid.' " (Kendall's references are: *Institutes* III and xiii.5; xi.7(twice); and for the idea of "a passive work," *Comm.* John 6:29.)

The present writer is in firm harmony with Calvin's perspective on the nature and essence of saving faith. I believe it to be the true Biblical concept of faith. What I charge is simply this: That the doctrine of faith which is generally found in

Reformed theology and in "lordship salvation" is *contrary to the Bible, counter-reformational* in nature, and *in sharp conflict with John Calvin himself.*

Chapter 3

[1]Gerstner (p. 229) seeks to counter this point when he writes: "James 2:26 makes the point of the passage perfectly clear. All that James says is that, just as you cannot have a man without a body and spirit together, so you cannot have a Christian without works and faith together."

But what impartial reader would ever get *this* idea out of James's text? In no way does James say that one does not "have a man" simply because his spirit has left his body. What we have in fact is a *dead* man – which is exactly James's point. A dead man is produced by the departure of his spirit from his physical body. Just so, a person's faith dies (becomes like a 'dead man') when it ceases to be invigorated by good works.

Surely Gerstner would admit that if a physical body is dead, it was clearly once alive. But he wishes not to draw any theological comparison with faith at this point because that would contradict his theological premises. My point still stands: The idea that a dead faith can never have been alive cannot be extracted from the text of 2:26 or of 2:14-26 as a whole. It is pure and simple theology, unsupported by evidence. In view of 2:26, the text *might indeed* be read just as I read it.

[2]A. T. Robertson, *Studies in the Epistle of James* (Nashville: Broadman, n.d.), p. 94 n. 2, assigns to the article "almost the original demonstrative force." But this is *extremely* unlikely here when it is not even true later in the passage where the article appears with faith at 2:17, 20, 22(twice), and 26. Any student of the original language can examine James's text and see for himself that the article occurs with faith only when faith is a subject or has a possessive word qualifying it (as in verse 18). Otherwise there is no article. There is no subtle significance to the article in 2:14! Quite rightly Dibelius rejects the special stress on the article: "Here Jas uses the article before 'faith'. . . but this is not to be read 'this faith', as many interpreters from Bede to Mayor have argued. Jas is not speaking of any particular brand of faith. . . The only attributive which is expressed. . . is this: faith which 'has' no works. But this is still the Christian faith and not an 'alleged, false faith.' " So much for building theology on an undetectable grammatical nuance! See Martin Dibelius, *James*, rev. Heinrich Greeven, trans. Michael A. Williams, ed. Helmut Koester, Herm (Philadelphia: Fortress Press, Eng. ed. 1976), p. 152.

[3]Lorenzen writes: "The original Greek makes it clear . . . that the rhetorical question calls for a negative answer: No! Faith without works cannot save! Works are necessary for salvation." Thorwald Lorenzen, "Faith without Works does not count before God! James 2:14-16," *Expository Times* 89(1978):231.

[4]Lorenzen, p. 234, holds that Paul and James cannot be reconciled. He is not alone in this view.

[5]This point is also made by Ropes, who writes of 5:20: "Note how here, as in 1:15, death is the result of sin." See James Hardy Ropes, *A Critical and Exegetical Commentary on the Epistle of St. James*, ICC (Edinburgh: T. & T. Clark, 1916), p. 315.

[6]The importance of a correct view of these verses is hard to overstate. Sanguine indeed is the opinion of Cantinat that, though verses 18-19 are very difficult – perhaps the most difficult in the New Testament – these difficulties do not greatly affect our comprehension of the text! The exact opposite is the case: these difficulties, if left unresolved, significantly block our understanding. Jean Cantinat, *Les Epitres de Saint Jacques et de Saint Jude* (Paris: J. Gabalda, 1973), p. 10.

[7]The evident unity of verses 18-19 as constituting the words of a single speaker is strongly attested in the literature on this passage. Many of those who have accepted this unity, however, have regarded the speaker not as an objector but as a pious ally who takes James's point of view. But this explanation is rightly dismissed by Davids because "no one has yet been able to find a case where this common stylistic introduction did not introduce an opposing or disagreeing voice." Peter H. Davids, *The Epistle of James: A Commentary on the Greek Text*, NIGNTC (Grand Rapids: Eerdmans, 1982), p. 124. Among those treating the two verses as a unity are: Robert Johnstone, *Lectures Exegetical and Practical on the Epistle of James*, 2nd ed. (Edinburgh: Oliphant, Anderson, and Ferrier, c1888), pp. 188-190; R. W. Dale, *The Epistle of James and Other Discourses* (London: Hodder and Stoughton, 1895), pp. 70, 71; so apparently R. J. Knowling, *The Epistle of St. James*, WC (London: Methuen, 1904), pp. 56-59; Joseph B. Mayor, *The Epistle of James*, 3rd ed. (London: MacMillan, 1910; reprint ed.., Minneapolis: Klock and Klock, 1977), p. 101; and Christiaan E. Donker, "Der Verfasser des Jak und sein Gegner: Zum Problem des Einwandes in Jak 2 18-19," *Zeitschrift für die Neutestamentliche Wissenschaft* 72(1981):227-240; and Francois Vouga, *L'Epitre de Saint Jacques* (Geneve: Labor et Fides, 1984), p. 87.

[8]Note this same format also in Romans 9:19, 20: (Objector) "You will say to me then, 'Why does. . . ?' " (Response): "But indeed, O man, who are you to reply against God? Will the thing formed . . . ?" The use of such structural markers as "but someone will say" and sharp-toned epithets directed at a senseless or ungodly interlocutor are well-known features of the diatribe style so prevalent in James's and Paul's day. For references see Mayor, pp. 99 and 102; Ropes, pp. 208 and 216; Davids, pp. 123 and 126 (bibliographic data in nn.5 and 7).

[9]See also the author's "Light on James Two from Textual Criticism," *Bibliotheca Sacra* 120(1963):341-350. As can be seen from nn. 7 and 8 above, the decision to treat verses 18, 19 as the words of a single speaker is not based on whether "by" or "without" is to be read in verse 18.

[10]The use of the challenge to "show me" in an ironical sense is well documented by Dibelius, pp. 154-155 n. 29. Especially parallel to James is a passage from *Ad Autolycus* 1.2, in which the apologist Theophilus writes: "But even if you should say, 'Show me your God', I too might say to you, 'Show me your Man and I also will show you my God.' " But this same ironic and unfulfillable demand is frequent in Epictetus, for example in the biting scorn of *Discourses* 3.22.99: "Who in the world are you? The bull of the herd or the queen of the beehive? Show me the symbols of your rulership!" For additional examples see Dibelius.

[11]The Greek phrase (*kalos poieis*) is taken by us in the sense of "do good," "do right," which seems the most appropriate sense in Matthew 5:44; 12:12; Luke 6:27. It is also viable in Acts 10:33 ("you did the right thing to come") and even in James 2:8 ("If you keep the royal law . . . you are doing what's right"). Attention should be given also to the secular examples cited by Mayor, p. 101. In Hellenistic Greek one would be unwise to insist pedantically on the good/well differentiation so dear to strict English grammarians!

[12]The word "alone," or "only," in Greek is adverbial in form and ought not to be taken as a modifier of "faith" in the sense of "by faith alone." This point is often ignored by writers. However, Lange grants that the Greek word for "alone" might be connected with the word "justified" in the sense, " 'not only by faith but by works a man is justified'," but he argues that in fact it ought to be joined "adjectively" with the word "faith." But in the New Testament, when the word *monos* ("alone") modifies a noun it normally has formal concord with the noun. The adverbial use is the only natural one here, i.e., "You see then that a man is justified by works, and not only (justified) by faith." See J. P. Lange, *The Epistle General of James* in his *A Commentary on the Holy Scriptures: Critical, Doctrinal and Homiletical, with*

Special Reference to Ministers and Students (New York: Charles Scribner, 1869), p. 87.

[13]Some have indeed sought a reconciliation between James and Paul in terms of differing concepts of works. Some time ago Lenski expressed a distinction that has often been asserted in one form or another. He states: "Paul and James deal with different kinds of works. Paul deals with law-works, which have nothing to do with true Gospel-faith . . . James deals with Gospel-works, which ever evidence the presence of Gospel-faith . . . " R. C. H. Lenski, *The Interpretation of the Epistle to the Hebrews and of the Epistle of James* (Columbus, OH: Lutheran Book Concern, 1938), p. 587. But this distinction is without foundation and has been effectively criticized by Douglas J. Moo in " 'Law', 'Works of the Law' and Legalism in Paul," *Westminster Theological Journal* 45(1983):73-100. As we have already seen (chapter 1 n.2) Calvin encountered this same argument from the "sophists" and rejects it (*Institutes* III.xi.14).

[14]About the statement in verse 22 ("by works faith was made perfect"), Adamson aptly observes: "The force of the statement seems to be that faith is fulfilled, strengthened, and matured by exercise." James B. Adamson, *The Epistle of James*, NIC (Grand Rapids: Eerdmans, 1976), p. 130.

[15]Hort explains "the Scripture was fulfilled" (verse 23) as follows: "The Divine word spoken is conceived of as receiving a completion so to speak in acts or events which are done or come to pass in accordance with it. The idea of filling, or giving fulness to, is always contained in the biblical use of fulfilling, though not always in the same sense." See Fenton John Anthony Hort, *Expository and Exegetical Studies: Compendium of Works Formerly Published Separately: The Epistle of James* (reprint ed., Minneapolis: Klock and Klock, 1980), p. 64. See also the stimulating discussion of Adamson, pp. 130-132.

[16]One must note Darby's comment on this passage: "James, remark, never says that works justify us *before God* [italics his]; for God can see the faith without its works. He knows that life is there. It is in exercise with regard to Him, towards Him, by trust in His word, in Himself, by receiving His testimony in spite of everything within and without. This God sees and knows. But when our fellow creatures are in question, when it must be said 'shew,' then faith, life, shows itself in works." J. N. Darby, *Synopsis of the Books of the Bible: Colossians - Revelation*, new ed. rev. (reprint ed., New York: Loizeaux, 1942), p. 361. This also is essentially the view of Calvin (see n.21 in this chapter).

[17]An indirect testimony to the depth of Rahab's vindication before men is to be found in the significant role Rahab played in Jewish legend. For specifics, see Sophie Laws, *A Commentary on the Epistle of James* HNTC (New York: Harper and Row, 1980), p. 137. Thanks to James, her name lives on in Christianity as a challenging role-model for every born-again believer who, though already justified by faith, also aspires to be justified by works.

[18]The view that James is talking about a false, spurious faith has nothing to commend it. Even though he holds that final salvation is in view in James 2, Nicol is absolutely correct when he writes: "James's point is not that faith without works is not faith; as faith he does not criticize it, but merely stresses that faith does not fulfill its purpose when it is not accompanied by works." See W. Nicol, "Faith and Works in the Letter of James," in *Essays on the General Epistles of the New Testament*, Neotestamentica 9 (Pretoria:The New Testament Society of South Africa, c1975), p. 16. See his whole discussion here, especially the statement (pp. 16, 17): "Our conclusion is that in this pericope James is not discussing different kinds of faith – as the Reformed scholars we have cited assert; he emphasize that those who believe must do good works."

See also Plummer, who writes: "But St. James nowhere throws doubt on the truth of the unprofitable believer's professions, or on the possibility of believing much and doing nothing." Alfred Plummer, *The General Epistles of St. James and St. Jude* (New York: A. C. Armstrong and Son, 1905), p. 137.

[19]Strikingly on target are the remarks of Dibelius (p. 178) who writes: "But in all of the instances [in James] which have been examined thusfar what is involved is the faith which the Christian has, never the faith of the sinner which first brings him to God . . . The faith which is mentioned in this section can be presupposed in every Christian . . . [James's] intention is not dogmatically oriented, but practically oriented: *he wishes to admonish the Christians to practice their faith, i.e., their Christianity, by works*" (italics his). As far as it goes a better statement cannot be found in the literature on James.

[20]James 2:14-26 is also treated as unrelated to the question of eternal destiny by R. T. Kendall, *Once Saved, Always Saved* (Chicago: Moody Press, 1985), pp. 170-172, 207-217. Although Kendall relates 2:14 to the saving of the destitute poor person described in verses 15, 16, his perspective on the passage is not very dissimilar to the view I have taken.

[21]A word should be said about John Calvin's own treatment of James 2:14-26. To the surprise of some, perhaps, we do not find in Calvin anything that reflects the theological tangle into which Reformed theology has fallen. In two critical points, Calvin agrees with the present writer *against* Reformed theology. The two points are these: (1) justification by works does not refer to our justification before God, but rather before men; (2) our good works are not the basis of our assurance of salvation.

Calvin says these things plainly: "So when the sophists set James against Paul, they are deceived by the double meaning of the term 'justification'. When Paul says we are justified by faith, he means precisely that we have won a verdict of righteousness in the sight of God. James has quite another intention, that the man who professes himself to be faithful *should demonstrate the truth of his fidelity by works.* James did not mean to teach us *where the confidence of our salvation should rest* – which is the very point on which Paul does insist. So let us avoid the false reasoning which has trapped the sophists, by taking note of the double meaning: To Paul, the word denotes our free imputation of righteousness before the judgment seat of God, to James, *the demonstration of righteousness from its effects, before men*; which we may deduce from the preceding words, *Shew me thy faith, etc.* [italics in the text]. In the latter sense, we may admit without controversy that man is justified by works, just as you might say a man is enriched by the purchase of a large and costly estate, since his wealth, which beforehand he kept out of sight in a strongbox, has become well-known" (italics added except in the case specified). Calvin, *Comm.* James 2.21.

Neither does Calvin fall into the hopeless quagmire of talking about a "spurious" faith which simulates the real thing so that true faith can only be recognized by works (see quotation from Dabney in chapter 2 n.1.) Calvin will not give the name of faith to those whom he considers James to be attacking. He writes, for example: "He [James] is speaking of false profession, and his words make this certain. He does not start, 'If a man has faith', but 'If a man says he has faith . . . ' Plainly he implies that there are hypocrites who make an *empty boast* of the word, when they have no real claim on it." A few sentences later, he says, "Just remember, he is not speaking out of his own understanding of the word when he calls it 'faith', but is disputing with those who *pretend insincerely* to faith, but are entirely without it" (on 2:14; italics added).

Although I might quarrel with Calvin's exegesis here, at least he is consistent with the fundamental premises of his own theology. Since, for Calvin, assurance was of the essence of saving faith, he does not ascribe this "false profession" to any who have found that assurance, but describes those without works as *insincere* pretenders who make a *false* claim to faith. Thus he will also ascribe to such people only "an indifferent and formal understanding of God" (on 2:14) or "a certain uninformed opinion of God" (on 2:19) or "a bare and empty awareness of God" (on 2:23). This is a far cry from his own definition of faith as "a steady and certain knowledge of the divine benevolence toward us" which is "founded on the truth of the gratuitous promise in Christ" (*Institutes* III.ii.7; quoted in full in chapter 2 n.5). Calvin does *not* hold that faith must be subjectively verified *to ourselves* by works, but objectively verified *before men.*

To be sure, Calvin expected good works to be produced in the life of the justified, but so do I.

Chapter 4

[1] But some do admit it. See Gerstner, p. 210. See also the article by Samuel T. Logan, Jr., "The Doctrine of Justification in the Theology of Jonathan Edwards," *Westminster Theological Journal*, 46(1984):26-52, especially pp. 42-48.

[2] By "unconditional" we mean, of course, that it is freely available. Naturally one must "take" the water (i.e., "believe" in Christ) to have it. An unconditional offer in ordinary life certainly does *not* mean that something is given whether one wants it or not! "Whoever desires . . . " is precisely the phrase that marks the unconditionality of this offer (Rev. 22:17). The text means, "if you want it, you can have it."

[3] Westcott takes the faith mentioned in verse 30 as faith "in the fullest sense." Yet he contrasts this with the faith mentioned in verse 31, taking the latter to mean "the simple acceptance of a person's statements as true." But this forced disjunction between the believers in the two verses is a transparent overrefinement based on, at best, a grammatical subtlety and, at worst, on a non-existent distinction. The latter is the case as a comparison with John 5:24 shows (see our text). Brooke Foss Westcott, *The Gospel According to John: The Authorised Version with Introduction and Notes* (London: James Clark, [1978 edition]), pp. 132-133. C. H. Dodd was correct to say that the distinction in question is meaningless here. See his, "A l'arriere plan d'un dialogue johannique," *Revue d'Histoire et de Philosophie Religieuses* 37(1957):6.

[4] Both passages use John's consistent expression for saving faith (Greek, *pisteuo eis*). See my discussion of John 2:23 and 12:42 in "Problem Passages in the Gospel of John, Part 2: Untrustworthy Believers – John 2:23-25," *Bibliotheca Sacra* 135(1978):139-152. For an excellent treatment of the use of the verb *pisteuein* ("to believe") in John, see Richard W. Christianson, "The Soteriological Significance of *PISTEUO* in the Gospel of John," unpublished ThM Thesis, Grace Theological Seminary (Winona Lake, IN), 1987.

[5] Although Brown needlessly assigns verses 30, 31 to editorial and redactional activity, he does say, "Almost certainly the words of Jesus in this section were addressed to the same type of disbelievers that we have been encountering all along." See Raymond E. Brown, *The Gospel According to John:(i-xii)*, AB (Garden City, NY: Doubleday, 1966), p. 354.

[6] For essentially the same view, see Rudolf Bultmann, *The Gospel of John: A Commentary*, tr. G. R. Beasley-Murray, with R. W. N. Hoare and J. K. Riches (Oxford: Blackwell; Philadelphia: Westminster, 1971), pp. 343-344.

Chapter 5

[1] This view of 1 John seems to have originated with, or at least have been brought to prominence by, Robert Law in *The Tests of Life: A Study of the First Epistle of St. John*, 3rd ed. (Edinburgh: T. & T. Clark, 1914). It is very much the controlling

conception in J. R. W. Stott, *The Epistles of John*, TNTC (Grand Rapids: Eerdmans, 1964).

[2]But the link between the antichrists and the gnostics, or "proto-gnostics," is by no means a firm conclusion of modern scholarship. Brown writes: "Most scholars, including those who speak of docetists and of Cerinthus, suspect that the adversaries of I and II John had gnostic leanings; and some are content to designate them as gnostics. Gnosticism is notoriously hard to define; the gnostics were marvelously varied; and orthodox Christians used the term *gnosis*, 'knowledge', almost as freely as those whom they excluded as gnostics for proclaiming a 'so-called *gnosis*.' The complexity of the last issue as it pertains to Johannine thought is reflected by these statements: 'Eternal life consists in this: that they *know* you, the one true God, and Jesus Christ, the one whom you sent' (John 17:3); and 'Now this is how we can be sure that we *know* Him' (I John 2:3). All early Christians claimed to know God – how then did the claim of the Johannine authors differ from the claim of their adversaries?

"Some nineteenth-century scholars thought that the adversaries of I and II John could be identified with gnostic groups named by Irenaeus and the other writers against heresy. For instance, Pfleiderer thought of them as followers of Basilides (*ca.* 120-145), and Holtzmann referred to Satornil (Saturninus). Such associations often presupposed a very late dating for I John and have been abandoned today in favor of speaking of the adversaries as "proto-gnostics" who antedated the named gnostic systems of the mid-second century. (Indeed, it is possible in my judgment that the Johannine adversaries played a catalyzing role in the development of such later systems . . .). However, in speaking of the 'proto-gnostics' one has introduced the truly indefinable. How many and which features of later gnosticism need have been present for a group to be so characterized? For instance, very important in later gnosticism were such features as a series of eons intermediary between the supreme God and human beings, an evaluation of the OT creator God as evil, and the preexistence of the souls of the *pneumatikoi*, or spiritually elite . . . Yet no such features are apparent in the statements in Chart Four of Appendix I, which are the key to the thought of the adversaries of I and II John."

See Raymond E. Brown, *The Epistles of John*, AB (Garden City, NY: Doubleday, 1982), pp. 59-60.

[3]But this opinion is far from universal. Brown, *Epistles* (p. 608), writes: "Many scholars (Alexander, Brooke, Klopper, Schnackenburg, Schneider) refer it ['these things'] to 5:1-12 or to the last verse of the unit." One must also note Smalley's comments arguing that 5:13 concludes a unit covering 5:5-13 and he appropriately points to an *inclusio* [a technique for rounding off a literary unit] consisting of "a repeated allusion [vv 5 and 13] to faith in the Son of God." However, Smalley does not confine the reference of verse 13 to verses 5-12 alone, although he admits that "these things" "may refer to John's teaching in vv. 5-12." Stephen S. Smalley, *1,2,3 John*, WBC (Waco, TX: Word Books, 1984), pp. 289-290.

[4]Commenting on verse 3 and the words "that you also may have fellowship with us," Smalley (p. 11) correctly observes: "In the second part of this verse John moves on to declare his purpose in writing."

[5]The range of the word for "fellowship" (Greek= *koinonia*) is well presented by Smalley (p. 12): " 'Fellowship' . . . is a richly significant theological term. The Gr. word literally means 'joint ownership', or 'partnership.' In the NT this 'mutual sharing' may refer to participation in either material goods, as when Christians in Macedonia and Achaia 'raised a common fund' . . . for the poor among the saints in Jerusalem (Rom 15:26); or in spiritual benefits, as when Paul speaks of 'sharing' . . . in the blessings of the gospel (1 Cor 9:23), or enjoying – in the words of 'the Grace' – the 'fellowship of the Spirit' (2 Cor 13:13; cf. also Rom 15:27)."

With this in mind, then, 'fellowship' between the believer and his heavenly Father refers to an experience of 'sharing.' At its most basic level what is shared is 'light.' God both is, and is *in*, the light (1 John 1:5,7). When the believer "lives"

(= "walks") there, he shares with God whatever the light may reveal to him. But this requires openness and a readiness to confess sins as the light may show them to us.

[6]Smalley's view of the text (2:19) bears considerable resemblance to our own. He writes (p. 103): "This raises the question of the initial status of the schismatics [= the antichrists]. It is certainly true that by the time of 1 John the erroneous theology, and indeed behavior, of the heretically inclined members of John's church had become apparent; and, of course, we must always be alert to the distinction between true and false claims to the faith within any Christian society . . . But it is possible, in this instance, that those who later allowed their heretical thought and actions to run away with them (when it could obviously be said . . . 'they were not of us') were in the first place believers with a genuine, if uninformed, faith in Jesus."

[7]Modern critical editions of the Greek New Testament (Aland[26], UBS[3]) read another form of condition which commentators often adopt. Morris is perceptive, however, when he writes: "The conditional construction implies that the disciples have not really known Christ and accordingly that they have not known the Father. In a sense, of course, they had known Jesus. They had known him [*sic*] well enough to leave their homes and friends and livelihood to follow him [*sic*] wherever He went. But they did not know Him in His full significance. Really to know Him is to know His Father. Up till now all has been preparation." In a footnote he adds: "There is another reading . . . This would make the words a promise: "If (as is the case) you have come to know Me, you will know my [*sic*] Father also." The attestation of this reading is inferior, and the context makes the rebuke more likely." See Leon Morris, *The Gospel According to John*, NIC (Grand Rapids: Eerdmans, 1971), pp. 641-642.

[8]Once again, Smalley's comments are observant (p. 238): "Love by itself cannot be the criterion for knowing God (v 7); and similarly a lack of love does not by itself prove that no relationship with God exists. But because God's nature is love . . . the knowledge of God *should* [italics his] lead to love for others . . . Anyone who enters into a real relationship with a loving God can be transformed into a loving person (see v 11)."

[9]C. H. Dodd expressed his own doubts some 45 years ago when he wrote: "Yet it is legitimate to doubt whether the reader could be expected to grasp so subtle a doctrine simply upon the basis of a precise distinction of tenses without further guidance. Moreover, it is not clear that this distinction of tenses is carried right through with the precision which would be necessary if the whole weight of the argument rested upon it." C. H. Dodd, *The Johannine Epistles*, MNTC (New York: Harper and Row, 1946), p. 79.

[10]What is called "aspect" in the Greek verb system is very poorly understood by many people who have studied (and written about!) the significance of the Greek tenses. The words of Zerwick are a caution frequently ignored. He writes: "NB: The aspects, as was said above, *present* the action *as* [italics his] a simple fact, etc.; the use of the <tenses> is determined not so much by the objective reality (*which commonly admits all three aspects according to what the speaker wishes to express* [italics added]) as by the speaker's needs: he will use the aorist for an action which objectively lasted a long time or was repeated, if what he wishes to express is simply the fact that the action took place; *or the present for an action which is of its nature momentary* [italics added], if what he wishes to express is the nature or kind of action as distinct from its concrete realization." Maximillian Zerwick, *Biblical Greek* (Rome: Scripta Pontificii Instituti Biblici, 1963), p. 78. The idea that the Greek present tense automatically suggests on-going or continuous action is a linguistic myth. No doubt it is believed by many (even some scholars) but it is mythical nonetheless.

[11]This problem was pointed out years ago by Dodd, *Epistles* (p. 79).

[12]As Brown puts it, *Epistles* (p. 403): "The logic of the statement [in v. 6a] flows from the preceding verse: there is no sin in Christ, and so those who abide in him should have no sin in them."

[13]One must be careful in 1 John 3:6b not to make the statement mean, "Whoever sins has *never* seen Him nor known Him." The Greek perfect tense, which is used in the verbs "seen" and "known," does not suggest this. The statement of Zerwick (p. 96) is helpful: "In essence, though not exactly in use, the Greek perfect tense corresponds to the English one, in that it is *not a past tense but a present one*, indicating *not the past action* as such but *the present <state of affairs>* resulting from the past action" (italics added). We could paraphrase the statement of the verse like this: "Whoever sins *is in a condition of failure to see and know* God." The impression left by this rendering is somewhat different than the one left by the English present perfects ("has not seen nor known"). The English verbs *can* imply "never" in the right context, but do not necessarily do so. If someone asks, "Have you seen Joe?" and the reply is, "No, I haven't seen Joe," this will normally *not* be taken to mean, "I've *never* seen Joe." Examples could be multiplied. The point we must get from 1 John 3:6b is that, *in the act of sinning*, a person has neither seen nor known God. That is, sin proceeds from darkness and ignorance toward God, never from a true "seeing" or "knowing" of Him. Sin, as it were, turns our eyes from God, or blinds us to Him, so that in committing it we can only be said to operate in spiritual darkness and in a profound lack of moral understanding. We are not talking about what our intellect may know – which can be much indeed. We are talking about moral blindness and moral ignorance, which is quite another thing.

[14]Very close indeed to our view is the view of Plummer who states (on 3:6): "By these apparently contradictory statements [i.e., 1:1-8; 2:27; 3:6] put forth one after another S. John expresses that internal contradiction of which everyone who is endeavoring to do right is conscious. What S. John delivers as a series of aphorisms, which mutually qualify and explain one another, S. Paul puts forth dialectically as an argument. 'If what I would not, that I do, it is no more I that do it, but sin which dwelleth in me' (Rom. vii. 20). And on the other hand, 'I live; yet not I, but Christ liveth in me' (Gal. ii. 20)." Plummer adds later (under 3:9): "The strong statement is exactly parallel to v. 6 and is to be understood in a similar sense. It is literally true of the Divine nature imparted to the believer. That does not and cannot sin. A child of the God who is Light can have nothing to do with sin which is darkness: the two are morally incompatible." Alfred Plummer, *The Epistles of St. John* (Cambridge: University Press, 1886; [reprint ed., Grand Rapids: Baker, 1980]), pp. 76, 79.

[15]The declining popularity of the "tense solution" is perhaps to be traced to the significant article by S. Kubo, "1 John 3,9: Absolute or Habitual?" *Andrews University Seminary Studies* 7(1969):47-56. The "tense solution" is abandoned by I. Howard Marshall, *The Epistles of John*, NIC (Grand Rapids: Eerdmans, 1978), pp. 180, 187-188. Raymond Brown, *Epistles*, writes of it (p. 414), "Alexander, Dodd and Prunet question whether the author would let such an important distinction rest on so fragile a grammatical subtlety. Would the readers perceive such a subtlety?" Brown also treats the view as contextually unsupported (p. 415). Smalley likewise rejects the "grammatical" solution and regards it as "stressing artificially the continuous element in the present tense" (p. 159); and he raises the pertinent question: "If God, whose nature remains in the Christian (3:9) and keeps him safe (5:18), can be said to protect the believer from habitual sin, why can he not preserve him as well from occasional sins?" (p. 160). Thus the "tense solution" is an explanation whose serious inadequacies are now widely recognized. Its true place in the history of the interpretation of 1 John is as an exegetical curiosity.

[16]The identification of the "antichrists" with "the children of the devil" is made also by Brown, *Epistles*, who calls them "the secessionists" (p. 416), and by Smalley who calls them "the antichristian secessionists" (p. 180).

[17]Brown, *Epistles* (p. 416), concurs with this analysis: "Structurally it seems to make better sense if ['in this'] refers to what precedes, while what follows (3:10bc) is seen as transitional to the next unit. The ['in this'] statement in 3:10a then becomes the conclusion of the whole apocalyptic theme that began with the mention of 'the last hour' in 2:18."

[18]The Greek expression *einai ek* ("to be of . . . ") is helpfully discussed by Brown, though not without some theological imprecision. Yet we can basically concur when he writes: "The main theological usage of *einai ek* is in the Johannine dualistic worldview to indicate origin from and/or adherence to one side or the other" (*Epistles*, p. 313). To put it plainly, we could say that 10b means: "Whoever does not do righteousness *is not on God's side.*" But this is not the same as saying that they are unsaved. Believers can choose "the wrong side" by choosing unrighteous courses of action. This is precisely what James warns his Christian readers about in James 4:4, for example: "Adulterers and adulteresses! Do you not know that friendship with the world is enmity with God? Whoever therefore wants to be a friend of the world makes himself an enemy of God."

[19]The same threefold division in 3:13, 14 ("the world," "you," and "we") is found also in 4:4-6 ('you," v. 4; "they . . . of the world," v. 5; "we," v. 6). It is thus easy to see the "we" of 3:14, which is quite emphatic in the Greek, as a third group, the Apostles, who are contrasted with the loveless world, in particular the "antichrists."

[20]Houlden comes very close to our position when he writes on 3:14 as follows: "V. 14 is ambiguous: but the last clause depends on the verb **know**, not on **passed**. So it does not mean that love brings about the transition from the sphere of death to that of (eternal) life (cf. i. 2; ii. 25; v. 11 ff.) – justification by works! – or even that the conviction that the transition has taken place is only held because brotherly love is observed to be present; but rather that the new life is savoured and enjoyed, and its reality assured, in the atmosphere of love which prevails. **We know**: not in the sense of intellectual demonstration but rather of experiential conviction. The love shows the genuineness of God's gift to believers, not because they are tempted to distrust it, but because they are concerned to show to those outside that this is their possession." This is a highly commendable treatment of this text. See J. L. Houlden, *A Commentary on the Johannine Epistles*, HNTC (New York: Harper and Row, 1973), p. 98. However, Houlden assigns verse 15 to the unsaved heretics (the antichrists).

[21]Brown, *Epistles* (pp. 445-446), has surfaced some parallels which are pertinent to the view expressed in our text: "This imagery appears in Jewish thought as well, e.g., Philo, *On Flight* 11 #58, 'What is good and virtuous constitutes life; what is bad and wicked constitutes death.' But in a general discussion on Abel, Philo, *That the Worse* 14 #48, warns of motion in the opposite direction: 'The soul that has extirpated from itself the principle of the love . . . of virtue and the love of God has died to the life of virtue.' Granted I John's reference to just/justice, the comment of the *Letter of Aristeas* is interesting: 'Injustice is equivalent to the deprivation of life . . . ' (212)." The death/life motif was both fluid and flexible in ancient thought. Modern commentators who are fixated on soteriology at every occurrence of the words "death" or "life" should broaden their horizons.

Chapter 6

[1]The statement under discussion is drawn almost verbatim from the Greek (Septuagint) translation of Numbers 16:5, except that Paul substitutes "Lord" for "God" (in Numbers). The Old Testament context suggests that the expression meant that God maintained His established relationship with Moses and Aaron despite the false claims of Korah and his rebels. The budding of Aaron's rod, which followed the judgment on the rebels, showed the truth of this claim by Moses. The line of Aaron was God's elect high priestly line. Dibelius/Conzelmann properly

connect the word "knows" in 2 Timothy 2:19 with election, and they write: "The latter [the use of 'knows'] was perhaps understood by the author, not mystically, but in line with the conception of the church and election. *Odes of Sol.* 8.14f also points to the origin of the first saying in Christian poetry: 'For I do not turn away my face from them that are mine;/For I know them;/Before they came into being,/I took knowledge of them,/And on their faces I set my seal.' " The quotation from the *Odes of Solomon* is too striking, and too appropriate to Paul's context, to be ignored. See Martin Dibelius and Hans Conzelmann, *The Pastoral Epistles*, trans. Philip Buttolph and Adela Yarbro, ed. Helmut Koester, Herm (Philadelphia: Fortress Press, 1973), pp. 112-113.

[2]It is often claimed by theologians that man has no capacity to believe and that faith, like salvation, must be given to him as a gift. But this view is contradicted by 2 Corinthians 4: 3,4 where Paul writes: "But even if our gospel is veiled, it is veiled to those who are perishing, whose minds the god of this age has blinded, who do not believe, lest the light of the gospel of the glory of Christ, who is the image of God, should shine on them."

From Paul's words it appears that Satan himself does not regard men as *constitutionally incapable* of faith. Instead, from his point of view, men are *in danger of believing* unless he actively blinds them! He must therefore prevent the truth from dawning on their hearts. This may be compared to an effort to keep light out of a dark room by (for example) drawing together a thick pair of curtains. The room *can* receive light but is prevented from doing so by the curtains. If someone pulls the curtains apart, light will automatically shine into the room.

God's role in bringing men to faith is therefore revelatory. (See our Lord's statement to Peter in Matthew 16:17.) As Paul puts it in 2 Corinthians 4:6, God shines His light into out hearts. Perceiving God's word as light (i.e., as truth) is precisely what faith does. When the truth of the sufficiency of Christ for the eternal salvation of every believer dawns on our hearts, at that moment we are *believing* the light and thus know that, in so believing, we ourselves are eternally saved. Thus faith is a capacity built into man by His Creator, just like the capacity to think or to speak. None of these capabilities is obliterated by the Fall, but man's use of them is seriously impaired by his own sinfulness. As a sinner, he prefers to believe a lie rather than the truth (see Romans 1:20-25).

Yet, despite man's darkened heart and Satan's special efforts to prevent man's illumination, God can break through all this darkness with the light of His truth and in so doing can meet a response of faith in man. So it is clear from all this that man's created capacity to believe things is awakened by the illumination God gives in the Gospel. Belief in the truth is impossible for any man so long as he remains persuaded that the truth is false. Once he is persuaded of the truth of the saving message, he has believed it.

Finally, one must say that the Reformed view that man is in every sense a "corpse" without even the capacity to believe the light when it shines forth to him is a gross distortion of reality. It is a transparent effort to press a metaphor like "dead in trespasses and sins" (Eph. 2:1) well beyond the legitimate parameters of that metaphor. Man is "dead in sins" precisely because he is separated from God's own kind of life, as Paul states in Ephesians 4:18: "being alienated from the life of God, through the ignorance that is in them." But the metaphor is seriously misused when it is made the basis for denying to man any and all capacity to receive the truth of God as light. If man had no such capacity, he could not be charged with sin for his unbelief, as Jesus told the Pharisees: "If you were blind, you would have no sin" (John 9:41).

[3]As Moffatt pointed out long ago about the Greek word for "tasted" (*geusamenos*), it "recalls the partiality of Philo for this metaphor . . . but indeed it is common throughout contemporary Hellenistic Greek as a metaphor for experiencing." James Moffatt, *A Critical and Exegetical Commentary on the Epistle to the Hebrews*, ICC (Edinburgh: T and T Clark, 1924), p.78.

[4]Moffatt, who rightly calls verses 4, 5a a "fourfold description of believers," defines "enlightened" as "in the sense of having their eyes opened (Eph 1^{18}) to the Christian God" (p. 78). See also Donald Guthrie, *The Letter to the Hebrews: An Introduction and Commentary*, TNTC (Grand Rapids: Eerdmans, 1983), pp. 144-145. His overall conclusions seem ambiguous (to me), but he is right to say: " . . . the words of this epistle . . . give no impression of incomplete enlightenment" (p. 144).

[5]The "falling away" described in Hebrews 6 is taken to refer to *Christians who apostatize* by Moffatt (pp. 76-78); Jean Hering, *The Epistle to the Hebrews*, trans. A. W. Heathcote and P. J. Allcock (London: Epworth Press, 1970), pp. 45-48; Hugh Montefiore, *A Commentary on the Epistle to the Hebrews* BNTC (London: Adam and Charles Black, 1964), pp. 107-108; and William L. Lane, *Call to Commitment: Responding to the Message of Hebrews* (Nashville, TN: Thomas Nelson, 1985), pp. 91-94. Lane, who believes (as do the other writers cited here) that the apostate will be lost, is as emphatic as anyone about the apostate being a Christian. He writes (p. 94): "The sin that the preacher warns his friends to avoid is commonly called 'apostasy.' It is a sin only a Christian can commit. *Apostasy consists in a deliberate, planned, intelligent decision to renounce publicly association with Jesus Christ*" (italics his).

[6]The comment of Jean Hering (p. 48) is appropriate: "Contrary to the majority of expositors we think that it is the same field which is being referred to, and that a comma should be placed after *'tou theou'* (end of v. 7), so that *'ekpherousa'* (= 'bearing') follows on simply from *'tiktousa'* (= 'it produced'). In that way the parable becomes less banal and very relevant, since it is an allusion to Christians who after having borne acceptable fruits become reverted."

[7]Hering (p. 48, n.16): "The custom of burning ground is expressly attested for antiquity by the Elder Pliny, *Historia Naturalis*, XVII, 300, #72, 'some people also set fire to the stubble in the field . . . their chief reason, however, for this plan is to burn up the seed of weeds.' " Moffatt (p. 80) cites Philo (*de Agric.* 4) as comparing "the eradication of evil desires in the soul to a gardener or farmer burning down weeds." But he misses the obvious relevance of this to Hebrews 4:8 when he adds, "but in our epistle . . . the burning is a final doom, not a process of severe discipline." But the untested theological assumption here is evident. What tells Moffatt that "final doom" is in view and not "severe discipline"?

[8]That the "willful sin" under discussion in Hebrews 10: 26-39 is, once more, apostasy, finds support from Moffatt (p. 149); Hering (p. 94); Lane (p. 141); Guthrie (p. 217); F. F. Bruce, *The Epistle to the Hebrews*, NIC (Grand Rapids: Eerdmans, 1964), p. 259; Philip Edgcumbe Hughes, *A Commentary on the Epistle to the Hebrews* (Grand Rapids: Eerdmans, 1977), pp. 418-19; etc. There is no reason to extend the list further.

[9]The concept of "sanctification" in Hebrews is well-stated by Hewitt: "The sanctified are those who have been made free from guilt through cleansing from sin and who have access into God's presence (x. 10, 14, xiii. 12). *Hagiazein*, 'to sanctify', has almost the same meaning as *dikaioun*, 'to justify', so frequently used by Paul. Denney [*The Death of Christ*, p. 126] draws attention to this similarity and then goes on to say: 'The sanctification of the one writer is the justification of the other . . .' " Thomas Hewitt, *The Epistle to the Hebrews*, TNTC (Grand Rapids: Eerdmans, 1960), p. 71.

[10]For this view see, for example, Roger Nicole, "Some Comments on Hebrews 6:4-6 and the Doctrine of the Perseverance of the Saints," *Current Issues in Biblical and Patristic Interpretation*, ed. Gerald F. Hawthorne (Grand Rapids: Eerdmans, 1975), p. 356 n.1.

[11]Among commentators who agree that the phrase "by which he was sanctified" refers to an actual sanctification of the Christian/apostate, we should probably include: Moffatt (p. 151); Hering (pp. 92, 94); Montefiore (p. 179); Guthrie (p. 219); Lane (p. 142). The sanctification is treated as simply claimed and not experienced by Hughes (p. 423); Hewitt (p. 362); R. Nicole (p. 362). Bruce (p. 259) seems ambiguous. But the text declares the person's sanctification as a basis for the severe retribution. The text says nothing of a "claimed" sanctification, which would be less serious. The greatness of the benefit to the apostate is precisely the point of the phrase. This would be obvious if it were not for the theological presuppositions that have been brought to the passage.

[12]As Moffatt (p. 158) states: "The aim of the change [from the Old Testament text] was to make it clear, as it was not clear in the LXX, that the subject of ['draw back'] was ['the just one'], and also to make the warning against apostasy the climax."

[13]Montefiore (p. 185) notes: "To **take no pleasure in** someone is tantamount to condemnation (cf. x. 6)."

[14]Moffatt (p. 158) observes: "[*Peripoiesis*] occurs three times in the LXX (2 Ch 14[13], Hag 2[9], Mal 3[17]) and several times in the NT, but never with [*psuches*], though the exact phrase was known to classical Greek as an equivalent for *saving one's own life*" (emphasis added). For references, see Hering, p. 97 n.28.

[15]G. H. Lang sees this text as we do. He writes: "Obviously this [Luke 17:33] agrees exactly with the warnings already considered that believers may be cut short by premature death and thus lose their life. It will therefore harmonize with the Lord's words should our passage [Heb. 10:39] be rendered, 'we are of them who have faith unto the *keeping safe of life*' " (italics his). See G. H. Lang, *The Epistle to the Hebrews* (London: Paternoster Press, 1951; [reprint ed., Miami Springs: Conley and Schoettle, 1985]), p. 193.

[16]Moulton and Milligan state of *metochos*: "This adj. in the sense of 'sharer', 'partner', as in Lk 5[7] (cf. Heb 3[14]) is common in the papyri . . . " James Hope Moulton and George Milligan, *The Vocabulary of the Greek Testament Illustrated from the Papyri and Other Non-Literary Sources* (Grand Rapids: Eerdmans, 1960), p. 406.

[17]Govett rightly links 3:14 with 1:9 where the Greek word for "partner" (="fellows" or "companions" in Govett) is used. See Robert Govett, *Govett on Hebrews* (London, 1884; [reprint ed., Miami Springs: Conley and Schoettle, 1981]), pp. 87-88.

[18]G. H. Lang, who believed strongly in free grace, held that the term "house" in Hebrews 3:6 referred to the indwelling of God in believers or in the local church. He believed also that God's indwelling could be withdrawn, although those from whom it was withdrawn remained God's people (= saved). We cannot agree that the Spirit's indwelling can be withdrawn from a believer (see Eph. 1:12-14; Rom. 8:9). Yet Lang's approach to Heb. 3:1 is essentially like our own. See Lang, *Hebrews*, pp. 68-71.

[19]As Dibelius/Conzelmann (p. 34) observe: "The purpose here is 'education through punishment' . . . which wants to prevent blasphemy (whether such blasphemy is seen as false teaching or, possibly, in the mere fact of opposition)."

Chapter 7

[1]See the quotations from Robert L. Dabney in chapter 2, n.1.

[2]We share John Calvin's view of Galatians 6:8 as dealing with the subject of *rewards*, and does not treat this verse as any kind of "test" of salvation! Let us hear Calvin on this verse, as he comments on the phrase, "*But he that soweth unto the spirit*: By 'the spirit' I understand the spiritual life, to which they are said to sow who look to heaven rather than to earth and who so direct their lives as to aspire to the kingdom of God. *Therefore they will reap in heaven the incorruptible fruit of their endeavours.* He calls them spiritual endeavours on account of their end, although in some cases they are external and relate to the body. This is so here, where he is dealing with the support of pastors. If the Papists try, in their usual way, to build on these words the righteousness of works, we have shown elsewhere how easily their absurdities can be refuted. Although eternal life is a *reward*, it does not follow that we are justified by works or that works merit salvation. The fact that God so honours the works which He grants us freely as to promise them an *undeserved reward* is itself of grace.

"If a more complete solution is required, then first I deny that in us there are any good works which God *rewards* except those which we have from His grace. Secondly, I say that the good works which we perform by the guidance and direction of the Holy Spirit are the freely granted fruits of adoption. Third, I say that they are not only unworthy of the smallest and meanest reward but deserve to be wholly condemned, because they are always spattered and stained with many blemishes; and what agreement have pollutions with the presence of God? Fourthly, I say that even if reward had been promised to works a thousand time, it is due only to the perfect fulfillment of the whole law. And we are all far from that perfection. Now let the Papists go and try to break their way into heaven by the merit of works! We gladly agree with Paul and the whole of Scripture in acknowledging that we can do nothing but by the free gift of God, *and yet the requital made to our works receives the name of reward.*" Calvin, *Comm.* Galatians 6:8 (italics added).

Clearly Calvin's comments are evangelical to the core. We find nothing here of the Reformed doctrine that works test the genuineness of our faith. Indeed, Calvin was insistent that assurance *should not be sought* in our post-conversion works.

Bell nicely summarizes this fact of Calvin's theology: "As a general principle, Calvin emphatically warns against looking to ourselves, that is, to our works or the fruit of the Spirit, for certainty of our salvation. We must turn from ourselves to rest solely on the mercy of God [*Institutes* 3.19.2]. The Scholastics taught that the Christian should look to works and to the virtues of righteousness as proof of salvation [as does Reformed theology today!]. However, Calvin rejects this exhortation to self-examination as a dangerous dogma [*Institutes* 3.2.38], and argues that we can never rely on such a subjective basis for assurance, for our sinfulness insures that we shall not find peace in this way. Forgetting the judgment of God, we may think ourselves safe, when, in fact, we are not [*Comm.* Rom. 5:1]. By placing our trust in works, rather than in God's freely given grace, we detract from his salvific work in Jesus Christ [Institutes 3.14.21; cf. 3.11.11]. If we look to ourselves, we encounter doubt, which leads to despair, and finally our faith is battered down and blotted out [*Institutes* 3.13.3]. Arguing that our assurance rests in our union with Christ, Calvin stresses that contemplation of Christ brings assurance of salvation, but self-contemplation is 'sure damnation.' For this reason, then, our safest course is to look to Christ and distrust ourselves [Institutes 3.2.23-4]." See Bell, p. 28 (The bracketed references are those of Bell's endnotes, p. 38).

Every one of these complaints drawn from Calvin can be laid at the door of Reformed theology today, which in so many ways is the modern counterpart to the Scholasticism which Calvin vigorously rejected.

[3]Bruce stresses the eschatological bearing of Galatians 6:8. He writes: "The eternal life is the resurrection life of Christ, mediated to believers by 'the Spirit of him who raised Jesus from the dead' (Rom. 8:11) . . . But its future aspect, with their appearance before the tribunal of Christ, to 'receive good or evil, according to the deeds done in the body' (2 Cor. 5:10), is specially implied here. Any one who did not seriously believe in such a coming assessment, or thought that the law of sowing and reaping could be safely ignored, would indeed be treating God with contempt." F.

F. Bruce, *The Epistle to the Galatians*, NIGNTC (Grand Rapids: Eerdmans, 1982), p. 265.

[4]Concerning the conditional clause in Colossians 1:23, Lightfoot remarks that the Greek particles (*ei ge*) "express a pure hypothesis in themselves, but the indicative mood following converts the hypothesis into a hope." J. B. Lightfoot, *Saint Paul's Epistles to the Colossians and to Philemon* (London: MacMillan, 1979; [reprint ed., Grand Rapids: Zondervan, 1959]), p. 163. Lightfoot's words are as far as the grammar can lead us and those who read more into the clause are misunderstanding the text. Equally plain is the statement of A. Lukyn Williams that, in the phrase *ei ge*, "the addition of [*ge*] lays emphasis on the importance of observing the condition, but determines nothing as to whether or not they will do so." See his *The Epistles of Paul the Apostle to the Colossians and to Philemon*, CGNT (Cambridge: University Press, 1907), p. 60.

[5]MacLaren's treatment of Colossians 1:22,23 is edifying. He writes: "No matter how mighty be the renewing powers of the Gospel wielded by the Divine Spirit, they can only work on the nature that is brought into contact with and continues in contact with them by faith. The measure in which we trust Jesus Christ will be the measure in which He helps us. 'He could do no mighty works because of their unbelief.' He cannot do what He can do, if we thwart Him by our want of faith. God will present us holy before Him *if* [italics his] we continue in the faith." Later, connecting vv. 28, 29 with 22, 23 (as we also do), MacLaren has this to say: "We found this same word 'present' in verse 22. The remarks made there will apply here. There the Divine purpose of Christ's great work, and here Paul's purpose in his, are expressed alike. God's aim is Paul's aim too. The Apostle's thoughts travel on to the great coming day, when we shall all be manifested at the judgment seat of Christ, and preacher and hearer, Apostle and convert, shall be gathered there. That solemn period will test the teacher's work, and should ever be in view as he works. There is a real and indissoluble connection between the teacher and his hearers, so that in some sense he is to blame if they do not stand perfect then, and he in some sense has to present them as in his work – the gold, silver, and precious stones which he has built on the foundation." See Alexander MacLaren, *The Epistles of St. Paul to the Colossians and Philemon* (New York: A. C. Armstrong and Son, 1897), pp. 107, 144.

[6]Meanings like "to take," "to take into possession," are found in Matthew 21:38 (NKJV), Luke 14:9, and (according to BGD, p. 423) in secular sources.

[7]Commentators long ago noticed a word-order problem in 1 Corinthians 15:2, when the verse is taken in the sense of "if you hold fast to the word which I preached to you." The problem is that, in Greek, the phrase "(to) the word which I preached to you" *precedes* "if you hold fast." (A minor problem is the sense of the Greek word *tini* which precedes "word" and is rendered as "that" by the NKJV and not at all by the NIV.)

One solution offered has been to connect the phrase "the word which I preached to you" with the expression "I declare to you the gospel" in verse 1. This yields the sense: "I declare (or, 'make known') to you the gospel . . . with what (=*tini*) word which I preached to you." But this connection requires a long leap backward in the text and is quite improbable.

The usual solution has been to make the phrase "with what (=that) word which I preached to you" the object of "if you hold fast" which follows it. This is not impossible by any means, but neither is it entirely natural.

It would be preferable to connect the phrase "with what word which I preached to you" with something immediately preceding it. In fact this can easily be done with the interpretation we offer in our text. The troublesome *tini* might be taken as an ellipsis for "what word it was which I preached to you" and may be shortened to, "the very word which I preached to you."

Thus the text can be read: " . . . the gospel . . . by which also you are saved, by the very word which I preached to you, if you take hold of (it) – unless you believed in vain." This is a clean-cut treatment of the Greek grammar and lexicography which avoids the puzzling word-order inversion required by the standard renderings of this passage. But obviously such an interpretation eliminates any reference to perseverance in 1 Corinthians 15:2.

For discussions of the problem covered in this note, see: Heinrich August Wilhelm Meyer, *Critical and Exegetical Handbook to the Epistles to the Corinthians*, trans. D. Douglas Bannerman, translation rev. and ed. William P. Dickson (New York: Funk and Wagnalls, 1884), pp. 341-342; and G. G. Findlay, "St. Paul's First Epistle to the Corinthians," in vol. 2 of *The Expositor's Greek Testament*, gen. ed. W. Robertson Nicoll (reprint ed., Grand Rapids: Eerdmans, 1970), pp. 918-919.

[8]The Greek words are different in each verse (15:2, *eike*; 15:14, *kene*; 15:17, *mataia*) but they are all functionally synonymous here.

[9]Interestingly, Barrett refers 1 Corinthians 1:8 to the doctrine of justification by faith. The term "irreproachable" (= "blameless," NKJV) is referred to the imputed "righteousness of Christ himself." Paul is thus "stating the doctrine of justification by faith without the use of the technical words he employs elsewhere"! See C. K. Barrett, *A Commentary on the First Epistle to the Corinthians*, HNTC (New York: Harper and Row, 1968), pp. 39-40.

[10]Very appropriately does Barrett translate "he will suffer loss" as "he will be mulcted of his pay." He subsequently remarks: "The servant of God who uses improper or unworthy materials, though himself saved, will miss the reward he might have had. We have thus already noted the next words, which are clear enough and need little comment: **he himself will be saved** (it is underlined that salvation is to be distinguished from reward, or pay; it cannot be earned)." One could hardly improve on this. See Barrett, p. 89.

[11]The hermeneutical issue here is about the "illocutionary force" of Paul's words. The significance of "illocutionary force" is aptly summarized by Hirsch: "Such an attempt at compromise [between intuitionists and positivists] can be discovered in the recent discussions of speech-act theory, based on the posthumous writings of J. L. Austin, who introduced into verbal meaning the concept of illocutionary force . . . Austin discusses how the very same word-sequence can have a different meaning by virtue of having a different illocutionary force. Thus, 'You are going to London,' could have the illocutionary force of an assertion, a command, a question, a request, a complaint, or an ironic comment on the fact that you are headed towards Bristol." Interpreters ignore this issue at their peril. See E. D. Hirsch, *The Aims of Interpretation* (Chicago: University of Chicago Press, 1976), pp. 25-26.

[12]The view that Philippians 1:6 has reference to the church's material support of the Gospel is a view with a long history, as Kennedy's comment on "a good work" shows: "De W. [De Wette, 1847!], Lft. [Lightfoot] and others refer this to [*koinonia*, 'fellowship'] of ver. 5." H. A. A. Kennedy, "The Epistle to the Philippians," in vol. 3 of *The Expositor's Greek Testament*, gen. ed. W. Robertson Nicoll (reprint ed., Grand Rapids: Eerdmans, 1970), p. 419.

Lightfoot on this verse writes: "By this 'good work' is meant their cooperation with and affection for the Apostle. By the workers of this work St. Paul doubtless means the Philippians themselves. Nevertheless it is God's doing from beginning to end: He inaugurates and He completes." J. B. Lightfoot, *Saint Paul's Epistle to the Philippians*, 4th ed. with additions and alterations (London: MacMillan, 1913), p. 84. Similarly, C. J. Ellicott, *A Critical and Grammatical Commentary on St. Paul's Epistles to the Philippians, Colossians and to Philemon* (London: Parker, Son, and Bourn, 1861), p. 7.

Martin, citing Lightfoot, writes: "It is possible to take *a good work* as an allusion to the Philippians' participation in the apostolic ministry by their gifts . . . " Ralph P. Martin, *The Epistle of St. Paul to the Philippians*, TNTC (Grand Rapids: Eerdmans, 1987), p. 62

[13]A truly commendable treatment of the concept of working out our own salvation (Phil. 2:12) is offered by Joseph S. Exell (b. 1849) when he writes:

> The *working out of salvation*: - I. A CHRISTIAN MAN HAS HIS WHOLE SALVATION ALREADY ACCOMPLISHED FOR HIM IN CHRIST, AND YET HE HAS TO WORK IT OUT. Notice - 1. The persons to whom these words are addressed. Through applying them to non-Christians they have been perverted to mean: "You co-operate with Christ in the great work of salvation, and you will get grace and pardon." But none save Christians have anything to do with them. They are addressed to those who are already resting on the finished salvation of Jesus Christ. If you have not done so, and are applying them to yourselves, remember that when the Jews came to Christ in a similar spirit, asking Him, "What shall we do?" &c. He said, "This is the work of God that ye believe on Him whom He hath sent." The first lesson is not work but faith, and unless there be faith no work. 2. But if salvation be this, How can we work it out? Salvation has four aspects. It means – (1) The whole process by which we are delivered from sin, and set safe on the right hand of God. (2) Deliverance from the guilt, punishment, and condemnation of sin, in which it is a thing past. (3) The gradual process of deliverance from its power in our own hearts, in which it is a thing present. (4) The final and perfect deliverance, in which it is a thing future. These all come equally from Christ, and depend upon His work and power, and are all given in the first act of faith. But the attitude in which the Christian stands to the accomplished salvation, and that in which He stands to the progressive salvation are different. He has to take the finished blessing. Yet the salvation which means our being delivered from evil in our hearts is ours on the condition of continuous faithful reception and daily effort. 3. The two things, then, are not inconsistent. Work as well as believe, and in the daily subjugation of your spirits to His Divine power; in the daily crucifixion of your flesh; in the daily straining after loftier heights of godliness and purer atmospheres of devotion and love, make more thoroughly your own what you possess, work into the substance of your souls what you have.

See Exell, *The Biblical Illustrator: Philippians* (reprint ed., Grand Rapids: Baker Book House, 1952), pp. 121-122. Exell's view is clearly compatible with our own.

[14]For a fuller exposition of this kind of teaching found in the words of our Lord, see chapter 4 in my book, *Grace in Eclipse: A Study on Eternal Rewards*, 2nd ed. (Dallas: Redencion Viva, 1987). For a definition of saving the life which follows the lines we are suggesting, see R. E. Neighbour, *If They Shall Fall Away* (reprint ed., Miami Springs, FL: Conley and Schoettle, 1984), pp. 29-30.

[15]It is legitimate to wonder exactly what Hort means in his discussion of "salvation of souls" (1 Pet. 1:9), but the present writer may be forgiven for thinking that Hort's ship might be "listing" in our direction, when he writes:

> . . . *salvation of souls*] In complete generality. Here, again, as I had occasion to say on *v.* 5, we have to be on our guard against interpreting the language of Scripture by the sharp limitations of modern usage. Salvation is deliverance from dangers and enemies and above all from death and destruction. The soul is not a particular element or faculty of our nature, but its very life (cf. Westcott on John xii. 25). The bodily life or soul is an image of the diviner life or soul which equally needs to be saved, and the salvation of which is compatible with the death and seeming destruction of the bodily life and soul. Here St. Peter means to say that, when the true mature faith possible to a Christian has done its work, a salvation of soul is found to have been thereby brought to pass, the passage from death into life has been accomplished.

See F. J. A. Hort, *The First Epistle of St. Peter, I. 1 – II. 17: The Greek Text with Introductory Lecture, Commentary, and Additional Notes* (London: MacMillan, 1898), p. 48.

[16]Cranfield, for example, prefers the view that the phrase "doing good" (literally = "good work") in Romans 2:7 refers to "goodness of life, not however as meriting God's favour but as the expression of faith." But this is wholly gratuitous. The text says nothing at all about faith, much less about works as the "expression" of faith. The context in no way supports this view, and Cranfield is guilty of reading his own theology (which is *not* Paul's!) into the passage. See C. E. B. Cranfield, *A Critical and Exegetical Commentary on the Epistle to the Romans*, Vol. I: *Introduction and Commentary on Romans I-VIII*, ICC (Edinburgh: T. and T. Clark, 1975), p. 147.

[17]Correctly, Charles Hodge writes: "When Paul says *the doers of the law* shall be justified, he is of course not to be understood as teaching, contrary to his own repeated declarations and arguments, that men are actually to be justified by obedience to the law. This is the very thing which he is labouring to prove impossible. The context renders his meaning plain. He is speaking not of the method of justification available for sinners, but of the principles on which all who are *out of Christ* are to be judged. They shall be judged impartially, according to their works, and agreeably to their knowledge of duty. On these principles no flesh living can be justified in the sight of God. The only way, as he afterwards teaches, to escape their application, is to confide in Christ, in virtue of whose death God can be just and yet justify the ungodly who believe in him" (italics his). *This is precisely the view I take of this text!* But I also extend it to verses 7 and 10 as Hodge (inconsistently) does not (pp. 46-48). For Paul, eternal life - no less than justification - is God's free gift (Rom. 5:18; 6:23). One can no more earn eternal life by "patient continuance" (that is, "perseverance") in doing good works than one can be justified by keeping the law. The reason? Because "there is none who does good, no, not one" (Rom. 3:12).
    For the quotation above, see Charles Hodge, *A Commentary on the Epistle to the Romans*, 19th ed. (Philadelphia: James S. Claxton, c1836), p. 49.

[18]Although his volume bears a *nihil obstat* and an *imprimatur*, the Catholic writer Karl Kertelge is on the right track when he writes on 3:9: "Here in verse 9 Paul is dealing in the first place simply with the general guilt of both Jews and Greeks. He now draws the conclusions of his previous argument: Jews as well as Greeks are guilty. In the preceding discussion, in 1:18-3:10, Paul has accused all, which means that all are under sin. This statement is the conclusion of Paul's whole exposition of human wickedness. That mankind as a whole is under sin, which men have helped to power by their own actions, is a final and conclusive argument for their need of salvation." Precisely! Those who interpret Romans 2:7, 10, and 13 as somehow validating the need for good works for final salvation, have left the stream of Pauline thought entirely and are shipwrecked on the shoals of a modern "scholasticism"! For the quote, see Karl Kertelge, *The Epistle to the Romans* (New York: Herder and Herder, 1972), p. 44.

[19]John Calvin himself took Romans 2:13 precisely as we have taken it. He writes: "The sense of this verse, therefore, is that if righteousness is sought by the law, the law must be fulfilled, for the righteousness of the law consists in the perfection of works.   Those who misinterpret this passage for the purpose of building up justification by works deserve universal contempt. It is, therefore, improper and irrelevant to introduce here lengthy discussions on justification to solve so futile an argument. The apostle urges here on the Jews only the judgement of the law which he had mentioned, which is that they cannot be justified by the law unless they fulfill it, and that if they transgress it, a curse is instantly pronounced upon them. We do not deny that absolute righteousness is prescribed in the law, but since all men are convicted of offense, we assert the necessity for seeking another righteousness" (*Comm.* Romans 2:13).
    To argue otherwise in Romans 2 is to seek to reverse the Reformation.

[20]John MacArthur criticizes me for making these statements. He writes: "As a pastor, I take issue with Hodges' assertion that Paul was unconcerned about the destiny of members of the flocks he pastored." MacArthur, *The Gospel According to Jesus*, p. 190. But MacArthur's phraseology employs a rhetorical "trick" by making it sound as if I had painted Paul as a detached and "unconcerned" pastor. The reader may consult the paragraph to which this note is attached to see, on the contrary, that my point is that Paul had "no reason" for such a concern.

Dr. MacArthur appears to be reading the modern church situation back into the first century. First, we must remember that none of the Pauline churches were mega-churches on the order of Dr. MacArthur's own. C. R. Gregory once calculated that the church at Rome, to which Romans was written, was probably about 50 people, taking into account the names mentioned in the greetings of Romans 16. In such churches the elders undoubtedly knew each individual and could easily ascertain whether he or she believed the Gospel or not.

But, secondly, Paul preached a Gospel in which assurance of salvation was of the essence of saving faith. As I point out in the text, Paul everywhere takes for granted that his readers are Christians and know it. Since MacArthur does not preach a Gospel that offers real assurance at the moment of faith, it is understandable that he should be constantly concerned about the eternal destiny of his membership. With such a theology, both pastors and their flocks must always be beset by uncertainty on this crucial matter.

[21]Romans 8:14 is best read against the background of 8:12-13. This writer has not found a better discussion of Romans 8:12-13 than the one presented by Anders Nygren in his *Commentary on Romans* (Philadelphia: Fortress Press, 1949), pp. 325-326. There he writes:

The Christian has escaped from that ruler, death. But the intention is that he is actually to *live*. If death has been deposed, we are to let it be deposed in our lives, and no longer shape our lives according to its demand.

We here call to mind again the dualism in the Christian life, to which Paul has referred again and again in the foregoing. In the sixth chapter, for example, he declared that the Christian is "free from sin"; and from that he immediately drew the conclusion that the Christian must battle against sin and all that would bind us to it. Out of the indicative, Paul educes an imperative. Through Christ we *are* free from sin; and *for that very reason* we are to fight against it . . . The same dualism emerges here, where Paul speaks of the Christian's freedom form death. Through Christ the Christian has actually been freed from death; but that does not mean that there is no longer any possibility for death to threaten him . . . The life of the Christian is still lived all the time in the scope of the first creation. He still lives "in the flesh," and there death has its chance to lay hold, when it strives to regain its power over him. Out of the flesh come all sorts of claims on him; and if he were to follow these, the result would be that he would be carried straight back along the way to bondage under death. It is therefore imperative to resist these claims and reject them as unjustified. Just as, in chapter 6, Paul was concerned to show that the Christian is truly free from sin, so that it can no longer come with any warranted claim on him . . . so he is now concerned to show that, in like manner, the Christian's freedom from death means that the flesh can no longer come with any justifiable claim. "So then, brethren, we are debtors, not to the flesh, to live according to the flesh - for if you live according to the flesh you will die, but if by the Spirit you put to death the deeds of the body you will live" (vss. 12-13).

So there are two different way to live. Man can "live according to the flesh" or "live according to the Spirit." As to the former manner of life, it must be said that it is not really life. On the contrary, in its basic nature it is quite the opposite. Therefore Paul says, "If you live according to the flesh you will *die*." In that case one does not speak of what is properly life. When we hear Paul speaking here about a life that is really death, our thoughts turn automatically to the famous words of Augustine: "Such was my life – was that life?" (italics in the original).

Obviously, this splendid exposition enables us to understand what it means truly to *live* as God's adult *sons*, who are led in this experience by God's Spirit. Christians who live at the level of the flesh and of death, are operating experientially far below their standing in Christ.

[22]Despite other grammatical possibilities, the view we have given in the text is precisely the view of the phrase taken by both Cranfield and Murray ("The obedience which consists in faith"). Yet both writers proceed to read their theology into the expression so as to extract from it a call to works. But in doing this, they are no longer exegeting the text at all. The phrase means no more than what it says: "the obedience which is faith." When one believes the Gospel, he has obeyed the Gospel, since the Gospel calls for a response of faith. See Cranfield, pp. 66-67; and John Murray, *The Epistle to the Romans*, 2 vols. in one (Grand Rapids: Eerdmans, 1959, 1965 [one vol. ed., 1968]), pp. 13-14.

[23]MacArthur wrote of 2 Corinthians 13:5 that this "admonition is largely ignored – and often explained away[3] – in the contemporary church." The footnote number (3) refers to an extended comment about a statement I made on p. 95 of the first edition of this book. In his comment MacArthur notes: "Hodges does not mention 2 Corinthians 13:5 or *attempt to explain* [italics added] what possible second dimension it might have" (MacArthur, p. 190). But this is fair enough. My silence *might* raise the suspicion that the text was too difficult for me to address. But the fact is, I simply underrated its importance to the discussion. I repair this error by considering the verse in this second edition.

[24]Although Ironside's view of the text is not quite our own, in its essentials it is extremely similar. Thus he can write: "In replying again to the suggestion that Paul was not a real apostle, he says, 'If you seek a proof of Christ living in me, examine yourselves.' Now if you take this fifth verse out of its connection you lose the meaning of it. Many people take it, as though he meant that we are to examine ourselves to see if we are real Christians, but this is not what Paul is saying." For his full view of the verse, see H. A. Ironside, *Addresses on the Second Epistle to the Corinthians* (Neptune, NJ: Loizeaux Brothers, 1939), pp. 282-283.

[25]Baird's treatment of 2 Corinthians 13:5 closely approximates our own when he writes: "In the intense light of the cross, the Corinthians ought to examine themselves (v. 5; *see 1 Cor. 11:28*). They have been putting Paul to the test when they ought to be testing themselves. The crucial question is, Are you 'in the faith'; is Jesus Christ 'in you'? (NASB). Faith is the original response to the Christian message (Rom. 1:16; 3:22), and the believer continues to stand in faith (1:24; 1 Cor. 16:13) and to 'walk by faith' (5:7). *This life of faith is characterized as life in Christ or Christ in you* – a life conditioned by the redemptive power of God (see Rom. 8:9-11; Gal. 2:20). Though the Corinthians may fail the test, they ought to be able to recognize that Paul has passed; the credentials of his service (11:23-29) are the suffering marks of Christ" (italics added). William Baird, *1 Corinthians; 2 Corinthians*, Knox Preaching Guides, ed. John H. Hayes (Atlanta: John Knox Press, 1980), p. 109.

[26]It should be a major embarrassment to Reformed theologians to discover that their treatment of 2 Corinthians 13:5 was completely unknown to Calvin himself. As we have pointed out elsewhere in these notes (see footnote 2 in this chapter), Calvin did not believe in testing the reality of our salvation by examining our works. Moreover, he regarded such an idea as a dangerous dogma [*Institutes* 3.2.38]. Naturally he did not find this "dangerous dogma" in 2 Corinthians 13:5! Let us hear his own words:

5. *Try your own selves.* He confirms what he has just said, that
Christ's power has appeared openly in his ministry. He calls them to
judge of this by looking into themselves and acknowledging what they
have received from Him. Firstly, since there is but one Christ, it is
necessary that He should dwell both in minister and people, and if he
dwell in the people, how shall He deny Himself in the minister? Further,
He had shown His power in Paul's preaching so clearly and
unambiguously that the Corinthians could not doubt it, unless they were
completely foolish. For how had faith come to them, and Christ and
everything else besides? It is with good reason that they are called to look
into themselves, that they may discover there what they despise as a
thing unknown. The only true and well founded confidence a minister
has is that he should be able to appeal to the consciences of those he has
taught for approval of his teaching, so that if they have anything of
Christ and of sincere godliness, they may be obliged to acknowledge his
faithfulness. This, as we can now see, is Paul's purpose here. But there
are two reasons that make this passage worthy of special attention.
First, it shows the relationship between the people's faith and the
minister's preaching: for the preacher is the mother who conceives and
brings forth, and faith is the daughter who ought to be mindful of her
origin. Second, *this passage serves to prove the assurance of faith* [italics
added], a doctrine which the sophists of the Sorbonne have so corrupted
for us that it is now almost uprooted from the minds of men. They hold
that it is rash temerity to be persuaded that we are members of Christ
and have Him dwelling in us, and they bid us rest content with a moral
conjecture, which is a mere opinion, so that our consciences remain
perpetually undecided and perplexed. But what does Paul say here? *He
declares that those who doubt their possession of Christ are reprobates*
[italics added]. Let us therefore understand that the only true faith is
that which allows us to rest in God's grace, not with a dubious opinion but
with firm and steadfast assurance" [italics added]. *See Comm.* 2
Corinthians 13:5.
It would be hard for Calvin to make any clearer his fundamental theological
stance that *assurance is of the essence of saving faith.* The distortion of Paul's text
into an appeal to confirm one's faith because true faith cannot be verified apart from
works, makes a mockery of one of Calvin's most settled convictions. The Reformed
treatment of 2 Corinthians 13:5 subverts Biblical assurance no less than did "the
sophists of the Sorbonne" against whom Calvin so vigorously protested.

[27]W. Nicol's statements are commendable for their frankness, if not for their
theology, when he writes: "Logically, then, good works must be a condition of
justification . . . " and, "From this it is clear that Paul might say: you must do good
works, otherwise in the end God will not justify you." See "Faith and Works in the
Letter of James," in *Essays in the General Epistles of the New Testament,*
Neotestamentica 9 (Pretoria:The New Testament Society of South Africa, c1975),
p. 22.

[28]What we allege here is to be carefully noted. The faith/works synthesis which
makes 'works' an inherent or implicit part of 'faith' so that 'works' are indeed a
"condition" for salvation (e.g., Gerstner, p. 210), does NOT represent the Reformers'
view of faith and works. Even when the Reformers insisted on good works as an
outgrowth of faith, they did not make 'works' a part of faith or a "condition" for
salvation. It might indeed be argued that the Reformers left a measure of tension
between their doctrines of faith and works. But Reformed theology's solution to this
tension is neither Biblical nor reformational. The Reformers themselves would have
been horrified by the resulting theology. For them, good works were never the test
of true faith, but rather, good works flowed out of *the assurance of salvation* which
was inseparable from true saving faith.
This is precisely the position of this book.

A strong case can be made that Reformed soteriology and "lordship salvation" are nothing more than a return to the Medieval Roman Catholic concept of "formed faith" (*fides formata*), in which faith is not effective for justification apart from works. See Paul Holloway, "A Return to Rome: Lordship Salvation's Doctrine of Faith," *Journal of the Grace Evangelical Society* 4(2, 1991):13-21.

Chapter 8

[1]Brown holds open the questions about (1) whether John 3 represents an historical scene, and (2) whether the words "of water" belong to the original text. Yet he has some helpful comments: "A second argument against the originality of the phrase 'of water' is theological. The objection that Nicodemus could not have understood the phrase and that therefore it was not part of the original tradition is weak. We have shown above that many of the OT passages which mention the outpouring of the spirit also mention water; thus water and spirit do go together. Moreover, several other passages in the Johannine works join water and spirit (vii. 38-39; I John v. 8), and so vs. 5 is not an isolated instance. If the phrase 'of water' were part of the original form of the discourse, then it would have been understood by Nicodemus against the OT background rather than in terms of Christian Baptism." Brown, *Gospel*, 1:142-143. Additionally, the kind of view I present in the text is recognized as definitely viable by Robinson, who writes: "It is clearly possible to take 'water and spirit' as a hendiadys, two terms for a single idea." See D. W. B. Robinson, "Born of Water and Spirit: Does Jo. 3,5 Refer to Baptism?" *Reformed Theological Review* 25(1966):15-23; quote is from p. 19.

Calvin likewise dismisses the baptismal interpretation in favor of the view that "water and spirit" both refer to the same idea. He writes: "Accordingly He used the words *Spirit* and *water* to mean the same thing, and this ought not to be regarded as harsh or forced . . . It is as if Christ had said that no one is a son of God until he has been renewed by water and that this water is the Spirit who cleanses us anew and who, by His power poured upon us, imparts to us the energy of heavenly life when by nature we are utterly barren." See *Comm.* John 3:5.

[2]The view that "of water" in John 3:5 refers to physical procreation is often suggested. Leon Morris (p. 218), who holds this view, writes that the "allusion [to physical birth] would be natural to him [Nicodemus]." But would it? Can it really be shown that this was a comprehensible concept for Nicodemus? Such extra-biblical evidence as has been advanced seems to fall seriously short of demonstrating that the suggested meaning is viable. But see the discussion in Morris, *Gospel*, pp. 215-219. For some of the proposed sources, see Hugo Odeberg, *The Fourth Gospel interpreted in its relations to Contemporaneous Religious Currents in Palestine and the Hellenistic-Oriental World* (Uppsala: Almquist and Wiksells Boktryckeri-A. -B., 1929), pp. 48-71.

The view that "of water" refers to physical birth apparently has no convincing parallel in Jewish sources. Thus it seems forced and artificially "clinical." The view of Brown, that the Old Testament would be the natural background for Nicodemus to understand the reference to water, is clearly a more likely position.

[3]Even the famous passage about baptism found in 1 Peter 3:21 is no exception. (In the text of this chapter we consider this verse briefly a bit further on.) But here we must note that Peter mentions neither "eternal life" nor "justification" anywhere in that paragraph (3:17-22). See also endnote 9 in this chapter.

[4]In the standard Greek lexicon in use today (BGD, 1979), the so-called "causal *eis*" does not even have an entry of its own. The lexicon merely mentions the claims made for it by J. R. Mantey in his articles and the rebuttal material by R. Marcus. For the references, see BGD, p.230, under 6.a.

[5]The view of Acts 2:38 which I give in the text was anticipated in its fundamentals by H. A. Ironside, who wrote as follows:

The Apostle Peter had just preached his wonderful sermon setting forth the life, the death, and the resurrection of the Lord Jesus Christ. He had particularly emphasized the fact that the Lord Jesus came to the nation of Israel in accordance with Old Testament prophecy as their Messiah, the One they had been looking for down through the centuries, but they failed to recognize Him when He came. They rejected Him and delivered Him over to the Gentiles to be crucified; but Peter concludes with this triumphant word, "Therefore let all the house of Israel know assuredly, that God hath made that same Jesus, whom ye have crucified, both Lord and Christ."

We need to remember that the word "Christ" means "The Anointed" and is the equivalent of the Hebrew term *Mashiach* or Messiah. Our Lord Jesus is God's anointed King. Men said, His own people said, "We will not have this Man to reign over us" (Luke 19:14). But God has raised up from the dead the One whom the nation rejected and He has confirmed His Messiahship to Him in resurrection. He has declared Him to be Lord and Messiah.

Now the effect of Peter's message was tremendous. We are told "there were dwelling at Jerusalem Jews, devout men." He was addressing himself not to the ribald crowd that had been in front of Pilate's judgment hall who cried, "Crucify Him, crucify Him"; but addressing primarily the devout Jews who were awaiting the coming of the Messiah, also a number of proselytes from the nations who had the same sincere expectations. And when these honest men heard Peter's proclamation, we read, "They were pricked to the heart." This was the work of the Holy Ghost. He so carried the message home to their hearts that they were deeply stirred.

There was no attempt to deny what Peter said. On the contrary, they accepted the message. Let us be very clear about that. Having accepted the message we can be very sure of this – they were *already born of God* [italics added]. The Apostle Peter tells us in the first chapter of his first Epistle, "Being born again, not of corruptible seed, but of incorruptible, by the Word of God, which liveth and abideth for ever . . . And this is the Word which by the gospel is preached unto you." These people had heard the gospel. They were pricked to the heart, they were deeply exercised; they believed the message, and that implies necessarily they had received divine light and were regenerated. They turned to Peter and the rest of the apostles and cried out in sore distress, "Men and brethren, what shall we do?"

We have quoted Ironside extensively here because it is hard not to admire the clear and methodical way this gifted servant of God builds his case for this view of the text. In the paragraphs that follow the quoted material, Ironside goes on to expound the force of the question, "Men and brethren, what shall we do?"

Essentially, Ironside holds that this was fundamentally a question about what they and their nation should do in the light of their horrible mistake. For Ironside, Peter's answer tells them: "Repent. Right about face! Instead of going on as a part of the nation that rejected Him, change your mind, and separate from the apostate group by taking your stand for Christ."

On the question of the forgiveness of sins in Acts 2:38, Ironside writes:

> You see, as part of the nation they were responsible for the rejection of Christ, and now Peter says, Change your attitude toward the Lord Jesus Christ and give this outward witness – be baptized in the name of the One you have rejected, and God will look at you standing there and you will no longer be under condemnation as those who rejected Christ, but you will be under His grace because your sins are forgiven. It was not baptism, but change of attitude toward Christ, that gave then forgiveness. The baptism was the outward manifestation of their hearts' new attitude.

Since the present writer was exposed to Dr. Ironside's writings many, many years ago, as a young man, I think it is probable that my own views developed out of the thoughts Ironside had expressed on Acts 2:38. Though Ironside himself cannot be blamed for any refinements I have made, I gratefully acknowledge my heavy debt to this thought-provoking discussion.

The reader will be rewarded by reading Ironside's entire treatment of this passage. See H. A. Ironside, *Lectures on the Book of Acts* (Neptune, NJ: Loizeaux Brothers, 1943), pp. 63-69. the quotations in this note are taken from pp. 64-65; pp. 67-68; and p. 69.

[6]For a full and very valuable discussion of Acts 2:38, see Lanny Thomas Tanton, "The Gospel and Water Baptism: A Study of Acts 2:38," *Journal of the Grace Theological Society* 3(1, Spring 1990):27-52.

[7]For Acts 22:16, see the follow-up study to the one mentioned in the previous footnote: Lanny Thomas Tanton, "The Gospel and Water Baptism: A Study of Acts 22:16," *Journal of the Grace Theological Society* 4(1, Spring 1991):23-40. In both studies, Tanton critiques alternative views with skill.

[8]The two most valuable defenses of the textual authenticity of Mark 16:9-20 are: (1) John W. Burgon, *The Last Twelve Verses of the Gospel According to S. Mark* (London, 1871; [reprint edition, Ann Arbor, MI: The Sovereign Grace Book Club, 1959]); and (2) William R. Farmer, *The Last Twelve Verses of Mark* (Cambridge: University Press, 1974). Though Farmer's conclusions are very tentative, yet his material is of considerable value.

[9]As noted earlier (note 3), in 1 Peter 3:21 Peter mentions neither "eternal life" nor "justification." The sense of the word "saves" is not to be taken for granted either. Furthermore, "baptism" need not be understood as referring to *water* baptism. The contextual stress on "Spirit" and "spirits" (3:18, 19) suggests that the analogy is with "Spirit baptism" and that Noah's entrance into the ark is seen as a visual image of our incorporation into the body of Christ (=the Church). We are thus preserved (=saved) from the eschatological woes of the Tribulation, since the Church will be delivered from these by the Rapture (1 Thes. 1:10; 5:1-11). "The days of Noah" are a well-known example in our Lord's teaching of the end-time events (see, Mt. 24:37, 38; Luke 17:26, 27). Although Luther understood "baptism" here as water baptism, he certainly lays the foundation for our view when he writes: "But we take ship in the ark, which represents the Lord Christ, or the Christian Church, or the Gospel which Christ preaches, or the body of Christ to which we cling through faith; and we are saved just as Noah was saved in the ark." *Luther's Works*, vol. 30: *The Catholic Epistles*, ed. Jaroslav Pelikan and Walter A. Hansen, (St. Louis: Concordia Publishing House, 1967), p. 115. How easy it seems now, centuries later, to bring 1 Corinthians 12:13 to bear on Luther's comments and to find in 1 Peter 3:21 no necessary reference to the sacrament at all. "Water baptism" lies behind this passage only in the sense that the physical ritual is a visualization of the spiritual reality embodied in baptism by the Holy Spirit. In treating the flood as a type of Christian deliverance from God's coming wrath, Peter can move directly to the true antitype for that, which is not water baptism but Spirit baptism.

However, no one can deny the truth expressed by J. W. Dalton, who has written a major monograph on 1 Peter 3:18-4:6, when he states: "3:21 is an extremely difficult verse, and we cannot hope to solve all its problems adequately in this essay." See William Joseph Dalton, *Christ's Proclamation to the Spirits: A Study of 1 Peter 3:18-4:6* (Rome: Pontifical Biblical Institute, 1965), p. 210. See his material on pp. 210-237.

Chapter 9

[1]It is particularly in reference to my discussion of heirship that some critics have thought that my ideas were without precedent in Christian literature. But in thinking so, they are seriously mistaken. Most of my suggestions on this theme were anticipated before the turn of the century by George N. H. Peters (1825-1909), who was born in Berlin, PA, graduated from Wittenberg College, and who pastored a number of Lutheran churches in Ohio. His magisterial three-volume magnum opus,

The Theocratic Kingdom of our Lord Jesus, The Christ, as covenanted in The Old Testament and presented in The New Testament, was first published in 1884 by Funk and Wagnalls, New York. I have used the 1972 reprint edition by Kregel Publications, Grand Rapids, MI, for the citations below.

Another significant volume which anticipates the contents of this chapter to a considerable degree, is G. H. Lang, *Firstborn Sons, Their Rights & Risks,* first published by Samuel Roberts Publishers, London, England, in 1936. I have used the reprint edition of Conley and Schoettle, Miami Springs, FL, 1984. I cite it below as Lang, *Firstborn Sons,* to distinguish it from his volume on Hebrews.

Although Lang held the view that unfaithful Christians, even though eternally saved, would miss the Millennium altogether, his analysis of the Biblical teaching on Christian accountability is hard to surpass.

[2]Peters, 1:570, writes most aptly: "Let the Davidic Kingdom be restored *as predicted,* and, in the very nature of the case, to verify the promises, the Theocratic king will also have *His associated rulers* assuring *the most perfect administration* of the laws, and securing *the most perfect government,* productive of peace, prosperity, and happiness, such as the world has never witnessed. The Word emphatically teaches that those thus chosen, accounted worthy of this rulership, are the saints. They are *'joint heirs'* (Rom. 8:17) with Christ, who graciously divides, without marring His own superiority and supremacy (but rather exalts it thereby), His own inheritance with them" (italics his).

Lang's words are equally apposite: "Joseph, David, Daniel, Esther became more than subjects under their respective sovereigns. Each attained to rulership and glory. It is for such supreme honour that God is now training the co-heirs of His Son (Rom. 8:17, II Tim. 2:10-12)." See G. H. Lang, *Hebrews,* p. 56. Following the quoted statement, Lang also writes: "A royal father may have a large family, but of these only a few may prove competent to rule in the kingdom and share its glory" (p. 57).

[3]It would be hard to improve on Lang's succinct statement of the central point of this parable. He says: "Upon the return of the nobleman he richly rewarded those servants who had been diligent and successful during his absence. And the special reward indicated is that *'authority over cities'* was given in proportion to their fidelity; that is, they were appointed to high places in the kingdom of their lord. And thus both the governmental authority and personal glory of our Lord He will most graciously and royally share with such as are accounted worthy of these dignities. And the degree of our faithfulness now will be the measure of our worthiness then." Lang, *Firstborn Sons,* pp. 58-59 (italics his).

[4]Green definitely has his eyes open when, commenting on 2 Peter 1:11, he writes:

> This passage agrees with several in the Gospels and Epistles in suggesting that while heaven is entirely a gift of grace, it admits of degrees of felicity, and that these are dependent upon how faithfully we have built a structure of character and service upon the foundation of Christ. Bengel likens the unholy Christian in the judgment to a sailor who just manages to make shore after shipwreck, or to a man who barely escapes with his life from a burning house, while all his possessions are lost.

Michael Green, *The Second Epistle General of Peter and the General Epistle of Jude: An Introduction and Commentary* TNTC (Grand Rapids: Eerdmans, 1968), pp. 76-77.

[5]Most appropriately Lang writes on 1 Corinthians 6:8, 9 as follows: "This warning is addressed to those of whom Paul could acknowledge, 'Such *were* some of you, but ye washed yourselves, but ye were sanctified, but ye were justified in the name of the Lord Jesus Christ, and in the Spirit of our God' (I Cor. v, 11). But now he has to say, 'Ye yourselves (the pronoun is emphatic: I am not talking of

worldlings, but of you same individuals), ye yourselves *do wrong* (adikeite), and defraud": "know ye not that *wrong-doers* (the noun of the same verb, adikoi) shall not inherit the kingdom of God?' Thus he asserts (1) that those who have been justified, sanctified, and washed from their old sins, may *do wrong* and *were doing it*; and (2) that *wrong-doers* (there is no article) shall not inherit the kingdom" (italics his). Lang, *Firstborn Sons*, p. 110.

[6]Peters repeatedly insists on the truth that only faithful believers will co-reign with Christ. Thus one of his main subject headings ("Proposition 90") states: "*Members of the Church, who are faithful, are promised this Kingdom*" (1:600; italics in the original). Again, he writes: "Only believers *are promised* this Kingdom. Faith and its fruits are essential to its inheritance. This is pointedly declared in Scripture, as e.g. Gal. 5:21; Eph. 5:5, etc." (1:601; italics his). Peters also recognized the possible loss of this privilege. Quoting a ministerial writer named Graff, Peters affirms:

> Graff ("Greybeard") in his "Lay Sermons," No. 6, truly observes that "the present or ecclesiastical dispensation may therefore be said to be allotted to the development of Christ's *aristocracy, the nobility* of His Kingdom, *the ruling class* in the world to come." After urging that humility precedes exaltation, he says: "If Christians were not forgetful of the distinguished honors which await them in the future, they would be less concerned about the honors and emoluments of the present." Pregnant words; but, alas, how few heed the lesson imparted. In No. 13 he has some thoughtful words on: "the Reward of Good Works that is superadded to Salvation," in which occurs the following sentence: "And although the literature of the Church abounds in 'crowns for the departed,' it is not improbable that there will be many crownless heads on the day when the Lord shall appear to receive them, inasmuch as the three crowns (whatever they may typify) designated in the Scriptures, are mentioned in each case as the reward of some special service or merit. (The 'crown of righteousness' to those that 'love His appearing'; the 'crown of glory' to those who feed the flock of Christ willingly, etc; the 'crown of life' to those who endure temptation and persecution.") Whatever may be thought of this attempted distinction of crowns, the idea of loss, of simple salvation [i.e., salvation without reward], is a correct one, as e.g. evidenced by the apostles' teaching in 1 Cor. 3:8-15."

See Peters, 2:591-592 (italics his). A couple of sentences later, he also says: "The unspeakable honor [of kingship with Christ] thus conferred explains why the demands of God in reference to supreme love to Him, unreserved surrender to His Will, etc., are, as required in this dispensation, not fanatical requirements (as unbelief suggests), but essential in view of qualifying the saints for this rulership."

It is not too much to say that, if such truths were widely known and taught in the Church today, the Church would not be so severely troubled by the doctrinal confusion which begets "lordship salvation."

[7]The intensely motivational character of this truth shines through in Lang's skilled articulation of it as he comments on Hebrews 2:5 ("For He has not put the world to come . . . in subjection to angels"): "In the purpose of God the *oikoumene* [world] of the future has not been put under the control of angels, but of men. This is a key thought, the resolving of many obscurities and perplexities which hinder believers from grasping the exact significance of the plans of God and the final and highest outcome of redemption. It is the key to some present enigmas also. At present God is not saving the human race entire and its affairs corporate, but is selecting from it the company that are to rule the universe, superseding the existing government. He is preparing for a complete reorganization of His entire empire, and is giving to these future rulers the severe training which is indispensable to fitting them for such responsible duties and high dignities. The Gospel has *not failed*, but is fulfilling the purpose God plainly announced, though not the end that many preachers have mistakenly proposed, namely, the conversion of the whole race. That general and most desirable betterment of this sin-cursed earth is in the plans

of God, but falls for accomplishment in the *next* period of the divine programme, not in this age. There is manifest wisdom in a great Leader first training a body of efficient subordinates before seeking to reorganize society at large." Lang, *Hebrews,* pp. 52-53. If there is a more elevating paragraph on this theme in Christian literature, this writer has not found it!

[8]Tatford clearly thinks in terms of litotes when he writes about the promise of Revelation 2:11 as follows: "True life lay beyond. In no wise should he be touched by the second death and the very form of the expression but emphasizes the certainty of that truer and fuller life." Fredk. A. Tatford, *Prophecy's Last Word* (London: Pickering and Inglis, 1947), p. 46.

[9]Again Tatford interprets through litotes when he writes this about Revelation 3:5: "Practically every city of that day kept a roll or register of its citizens . . . one who had performed some great exploit deserving of special distinction, was honoured by having his name inscribed in golden letters in the citizen's roll. Our Lord's emphatic statement, therefore, implies not merely that the name of the overcomer shall not be expunged, but *per contra* that it shall be inscribed in golden letters in the heavenly roll." Tatford, p. 63 (see pp. 62-63).

[10]J. William Fuller, " 'I Will Not Erase His Name from the Book of Life' (Revelation 3:5)," *Journal of the Evangelical Theological Society* 26(1983):299. He goes on to say, "Surely the burden of proof is on the shoulders of those who would argue that the warnings are not genuinely addressed to true believers as they seem to be and that the promises are genuinely addressed to all believers (as they seem not to be). Hence the 'overcomer' is the individual Christian who enjoys special benefits in eternity for refusing to give up his faith in spite of persecution during life on earth" (p. 299). Of course, this general view of the "overcomers" has a long and respectable history. See, for example, J. N. Darby, *Synopsis of the Books of the Bible,* 5: *Colossians – The Revelation* (Kingston-On-Thames: Stow Hill Bible and Tract Depot, 1949 printing), p. 380; William Kelly, *Lectures on the Book of Revelation,* new ed. (London: G. Morrish, n.d.), p. 36; Walter Scott, *Exposition of the Revelation of Jesus Christ,* 4th ed. (London: Pickering and Inglis, n.d.), pp. 64-65.

[11]Lang succinctly capsulizes what is central to this chapter when he writes: "Salvation from perdition is definitely without works (Rom. 4:1-8), and to teach otherwise is to falsify the gospel: but equally definitely ruling with Christ depends on works, as Rev. 2:26 states, and to teach otherwise is to falsify our hope, by putting it on a false basis." See Lang, *Hebrews,* p. 71.

Chapter 10

[1]Throughout the endnotes to this book we have sought to show how often the perspective of John Calvin is precisely our own. This was not an effort to validate every facet of Calvin's theology, still less was it an effort to show that Calvin agreed with our position at every point. Of course he did not.

But at the same time we were seeking to rebut the claim of many Calvinists today to stand in a true line of descent from this famous Reformer. What we in fact see in modern Reformed (or, Puritan) theology is a heavy retrenchment in the direction of the scholastic theology which Calvin himself vigorously opposed. So much is this the case, that to the modern ear Calvin's arguments against the "sophists" sound eerily as though they might have been spoken against Reformed theologians of the present day.

Of course, I do not expect this serious charge to be easily acknowledged by contemporary Calvinist theologians, but I am appealing over their heads to the general reader of this book. Read Calvin as carefully as you will and I am confident that you will find his fundamental position to be as we have described it.

Let these points be reasserted where Calvin differs definitively from Reformed theology:

(1)   Calvin held (against Reformed thought) that assurance of salvation is *of the essence of* (an essential part of) saving faith. This means that, for Calvin, a man who does not find assurance by believing has not really believed.

(2)   For Calvin, faith was essentially passive and was basically a "persuasion." Indeed, he can even call it "knowledge" or "illumination." Thus Calvin would never have subscribed to the 'lordship' view that faith is an act of the will involving submission and surrender.

(3)   For Calvin it was a "dangerous dogma" to hold that assurance could be sought in our post-conversion good works, i.e., in the fruits of the Spirit in our lives.

These claims have already been established on scholarly grounds by writers like R. T. Kendall, M. Charles Bell, and A. N. S. Lane (for bibliography, see chapter 2, n.1). We are now waiting for a candid admission of the facts from the leading theological spokesmen from the Reformed tradition. We already have Robert Dabney's admission (see chapter 2, n.2), but we don't have theirs.

How long will we have to wait?

Postscript

[1] Martin Luther, *A Commentary on St. Paul's Epistle to the Galatians, Based on Lectures Delivered by Martin Luther at the University of Wittenberg in the Year 1531 and First Published in 1535*, a rev. and completed trans. based on the 'Middleton' edition of the English version of 1575 (London: James Clarke, 1953), p. 98.

[2] *Rock of Ages*, by A. M. Toplady and Thomas Hastings.

[3] *Just As I Am*, by Charlotte Elliott and William B. Bradbury.

[4] *No Other Plea*, by Lidie H. Edmunds and William J. Kirkpatrick.

SCRIPTURE INDEX
(Compiled by Enrique Mendez)